This book is thoughtful, clear, pastoral, convincing, and convicting. It does not lead to a position that Christians should give less than ten percent. Rather, (a) if the foundation of giving is our relationship with God and the grace and love he gives us and (b) if the amount we give is based on our income, what we determine in our heart, the needs of those ministering to us and of fellow Christians, and generosity, then why give only ten percent?

Andy Naselli, Ph.D.
Assistant Professor of New Testament and Biblical Theology
Bethlehem College and Seminary, Minneapolis, MN

David Croteau has provided the Church a concise and helpful argument for a biblical approach to giving for modern times. By contending that God does not require tithing for believers today, Croteau does not seek to minimize the giving of God's people. Rather, he wants people to give in accordance to the pattern provided by the Scriptures: generously, cheerfully, and sacrificially. May God's people understand that we should not limit our giving to 10% of our resources, but to give in light of God's abundant mercy and grace toward us.

Michael A. Grisanti, Ph.D.
Professor of Old Testament
The Master's Seminary, Sun Valley, CA

With sharp simplicity, David Croteau exposes a range of assumptions that many Christians employ in their thinking about tithing. He demonstrates how these assumptions can appear to be biblically based, and yet surprisingly be flawed. Croteau then uses sound biblical principles to shape a wise and godly attitude towards financial giving for the Christian. His concern for biblical faithfulness and God's grace is evident throughout, and his explanations are enlightening and encouraging. Croteau is to be commended for serving the Christian community with these valuable (pun intended!) insights on what can be a controversial or even burdensome topic for believers.

George Athas, Ph.D.
Dean of Research and Senior Lecturer in Old Testament
Moore Theological College, Sydney, Australia

David Croteau has already published a detailed study of all the significant biblical, theological and historical evidence for and against tithing as a mandatory practice for Christians. Here he distills the highlights of that research in brief, accessible form, responding to the most common arguments for tithing. Croteau convincingly demonstrates that believers after Jesus' death and resurrection are not required to give ten percent. Instead they are exhorted to generosity and sacrifice, which for a few Westerners may be less than ten percent but for many of us means much more. Here is essential reading for the Christian who wants to be biblically obedient!

Craig L. Blomberg, Ph.D.
Distinguished Professor of New Testament
Denver Seminary, Denver, CO

There are many sound bites on tithing, but few exegetical studies - even fewer that are understandable to the average layperson, well-written, and concerned about the practical generosity of God's people. Well, there may only be one book that fits that description, and you're holding it in your hands.

Robert L. Plummer, Ph.D.
Professor of New Testament Interpretation
The Southern Baptist Theological Seminary, Louisville, KY

If you want a concise overview of a better way to give generously to the Lord, then this book is for you. Dr. Croteau has provided a resource for the church to examine biblical principles for giving today. He fairly responds to the arguments for tithing today, and winsomely presents his view of grace-driven giving. Whether or not you believe tithing is still applicable today, this book will help you sort through the issue, and become a more generous giver.

Russell S. Woodbridge, Ph.D.
co-author of *Health, Wealth & Happiness: Has the Prosperity Gospel Overshadowed the Gospel of Christ*

David Croteau has a Th.M. and Ph.D. in New Testament from Southeastern Baptist Theological Seminary and and is Professor of New Testament and Greek at Columbia International University Seminary and School of Ministry in Columbia, South Carolina. He has published four articles and contributed to the book *Perspectives on Tithing: Four Views* (Broadman and Holman, 2011).

The *Areopagus Critical Christian Issues* series examines important issues in understanding Christian beliefs and developing sound Christian practice. Each booklet is short — less than 80 pages in length — and provides an academically sound and biblically rooted examination of a particular question about doctrine or practice or an area of basic Christian belief. It is jointly edited by Dr. Allan R. Bevere and Dr. David Alan Black.

TITHING AFTER THE CROSS

DAVID A. CROTEAU

Energion Publications
Gonzalez, FL
2013

ISBN10: 1-938434-12-9
ISBN13: 978-1-938434-12-9
Library of Congress Control Number: 2013942939

Energion Publications
P. O. Box 841
Gonzalez, FL 32560

energionpubs.com
850-525-3916

TABLE OF CONTENTS

DEDICATION

To John MacArthur
For the thought-provoking foundations that have
culminated in over a decade of study on this topic

To David Alan Black
For providing the initial opportunity
to write and research on tithing

To Andreas Köstenberger
For encouraging and partnering with me
to pursue this topic in its fullness

FROM THE EDITORS

The Areopagus is a hill in Athens that was once the meeting place of a Greek council. Paul preached on that hill while visiting Athens, presenting the gospel to the Athenian council and converting one of them (Acts 17). It thus provides an excellent name for this series of booklets that examines important issues in understanding Christian beliefs and developing sound Christian practice. Each booklet is intentionally short – less than 80 pages in length – and provides an academically sound and biblically rooted examination of a particular question about doctrine or practice or an area of basic Christian belief.

The Areopagus series is orthodox in doctrine but not bound to the doctrinal statements of any denomination. It is both firm in conviction and irenic in tone. Authors have been chosen for their ability to understand a topic in depth and present it clearly.

Each book is rigorous in scholarship because we believe the church deserves no less. Yet the volumes are accessible in style as we also believe that there are many pastors and laypersons in the church who desire to think deeply and critically about the issues that confront the church today in its life and mission in the world.

In keeping with these convictions, the authors in this series are either professors who are also actively involved in ministry, pastors who have not only thought through the issues but whose ministry has been guided by their convictions, or laypersons whose faith and commitment to the lordship of Jesus Christ and his church have contributed to the Great Commission Jesus gave to all of his followers (Matt. 28:18-20).

The *Areopagus Critical Christian Issues* series is not only meant to help the church think differently. We hope that those who read its volumes will be different, for the gospel is about the transformation of the whole person – mind, heart, and soul.

We take the words of the apostle Paul seriously when he says to the Athenians that God "has fixed a day on which he will have the world judged in righteousness by a man whom he has appointed; and of this he has given assurance to all by raising him from the dead" (Acts 17:31).

Allan R. Bevere
David Alan Black
Editors

ACKNOWLEDGMENTS AND PREFACE

While pursing the M.Div. in seminary, I was first challenged with the teaching that tithing was not required for Christians. I studied the issue, debated with friends, and talked with many professors and pastors. When I completed my degree, I moved to North Carolina for more schooling. The topic still lingered for another two or three years. I finally wrote my thoughts down for a Ph.D. seminar I took under Dr. David Alan Black. His feedback and encouragement was pivotal in motivating me to pursue the topic further. Thank you, Dr. Black, both for that class and for asking me to consider writing this book.

I must thank my family for their patience in allowing me the time to write, mostly during the summer months. Thanks are also well deserved to the many "sparring partners" that have sharpened my thoughts throughout the years. Thanks to Dr. Andreas Köstenberger for all the help and guidance he provided during my dissertation work. Thanks to the Drowsy Poet Café in Givens Books and Little Dickens on Lakeside Drive in Lynchburg, Virginia, where nearly all of the manuscript was written.

For some of you, the closing chapter might raise a plethora of questions. If necessary, I may post answers to more specific questions on my blog at www.slaveoftheword.blogspot.com. Feel free to contact me with any feedback, comments, or questions you may have.

I

INTRODUCTION

I was recently on a radio show and an offended caller questioned the host, asking why in the world she would put someone on the air who was trying to deconstruct tithing. How on earth could that be edifying to the body of Christ? The caller was convinced that my ploy was to coerce people to give less! If you think my purpose in this book is simply to deconstruct tithing or to convince you to give less, you'll be sorely disappointed. "What is my purpose?" you may ask. Well, let me tell you. Through a detailed study of what Scripture says about tithing and giving, I hope to accomplish a simple objective: that people would seek God Himself in the intimate relationship He desires for wisdom regarding the amount they should offer as opposed to being burdened with a legalistic number. My hope is that people would be released through the knowledge the Bible imparts on the subject so that they do not give out of a guilty obligation but out of a cheerful heart, wisely stewarding their finances, overflowing in worshipful gratitude as they give their gift.

I have previously written on the subject of tithing,[1] so why another book? My previous work was more of an inductive study, comprehensively sorting through the biblical texts on tithing. This book is more deductive and much more of a compendium work than the almost 400 pages I previously wrote. Based upon my observations regarding this subject, I have encountered many specific arguments in favor of the requirement for Christians to tithe. While

---

1 See David A. Croteau, *You Mean I Don't Have to Tithe? A Deconstruction of Tithing and a Reconstruction of Post-Tithe Giving* (Eugene, OR: Pickwick, 2010); cf. David A. Croteau, ed., *Perspectives on Tithing: 4 Views* (Nashville: Broadman & Holman, 2011).

most of the information necessary to respond to these arguments is present in my other publications, it is not convenient to quickly access the data. Therefore, I hope to present the arguments for tithing and explicitly respond to them in a brief and easy-to-access layout. I want this book to be a most useful resource, one a minister or Bible study teacher could use to locate certain arguments and corresponding responses.

Here's what to expect. The book will travel through five categories of arguments used to support the requirement of tithing. Beginning with Scripture, Old Testament and then New Testament arguments will be discussed. Six arguments from the Old Testament will be examined, including the use of Malachi 3 and the narrative of Abram's encounter with Melchizedek. Six more arguments from the New Testament will be presented, including a discussion of Hebrews 7 and whether or not tithing should be done from one's income. There are six theological arguments, including the correlation between tithing and the Sabbath, as well as the argument that tithing is part of the moral, eternal law of God. An analysis of the two historical arguments for tithing will show that this issue has never really had uniformity throughout church history. Experiential arguments might seem unconvincing to some people on the surface, but the three discussed in Chapter 6 have been used by many to convince people of the obligation to give 10 percent of one's income.

There are many different reasons why the arguments for tithing fail. Sometimes they fail because the literary context of the passage is not adequately considered. This is the case with the argument based on Hebrews 7. At other times an argument fails because interpreters lack knowledge of the historical context or background that is necessary to understand the passage. Matthew 23:23 (cf. Luke 18:12) is an example of this. Some of the arguments from church history depend upon insufficient or ill-informed research on certain individuals. Martin Luther's stance on tithing has been misunderstood by many who have studied his views on tithing. Also, traditions and experience can sometimes cloud judgments or the way a text is read. It is difficult to get out of our preunderstandings, but it can be done with some effort. Maybe the most common reason these arguments fail to be convincing is that they neglect or forget the definition and description of tithing in the Mosaic Law, which is where our attention will turn now.

THE BIBLICAL TITHE DEFINED

When I first started studying the issue of tithing, I began by reading all of the verses in the Pentateuch to try and arrive at a clear picture of what tithing looked like for those under the Mosaic Law. I quickly became disheartened, as I had no clue how to reconcile the passages with each other. However, after much review, a clear definition of tithing can be arrived at that will aid in reading the passages that discuss it.

The word "tithe" means "a tenth." That is simply the dictionary meaning. It does not necessarily mean "a tenth of income" or "a religious contribution," even though that is how many people use it today. But looking up the definition of the word "tithe" does not inform us as to the biblical definition of tithing.

The definition of the tithe in the Mosaic Law is: giving 10 percent of one's increase from crops grown in the land of Israel or cattle that feed off the land of Israel. It was consistently connected to the land of Israel and never referred to an increase in capital that was gained apart from the land. Tithing was done multiple times during the year and the total amount tithed was at least 20 percent. How could the amount be at least 20 percent if the word means 10 percent?

In Numbers 18:21, the Israelites are given the command to give 10 percent of the increase of their crops from the land to the Levites. Leviticus 27:30 and 32 describe what items were subject to tithing: seed of the land, fruit of the tree, and animals from the herd or flock. This tithe is called the Levitical Tithe.

A second tithe, the Festival Tithe, is described in Deuteronomy 14:22-27. This tithe was to be used in connection with celebrating the three main festivals of Judaism: Passover, Tabernacles, and Pentecost (or the Festival of Weeks). Both crops and cattle are referenced in this tithe as well (cf. Deuteronomy 14:23).

A controversy exists about the third tithe: the Charity Tithe. It was given every three years and is discussed in Deuteronomy 14:28-29. Therefore, the following structure seems to have been commanded in the Mosaic Law:

Year 1	Levitical Tithe and Festival Tithe
Year 2	Levitical Tithe and Festival Tithe
Year 3	Levitical Tithe, Festival Tithe, and Charity Tithe
Year 4	Levitical Tithe and Festival Tithe
Year 5	Levitical Tithe and Festival Tithe
Year 6	Levitical Tithe, Festival Tithe, and Charity Tithe

However, every seventh year was a Sabbatical Year, so nothing would be required that year. The giving percentage was as follows:

Year 1	20 percent
Year 2	20 percent
Year 3	30 percent
Year 4	20 percent
Year 5	20 percent
Year 6	30 percent
Year 7	0 percent

This means that during the first six years, the average giving would be about 23 1/3 percent. However, if the Sabbatical Year was kept, then the overall average would be about 20 percent. And this only refers to the tithes, not the many other offerings required in the Mosaic Law.

Some interpreters have argued that the Charity Tithe replaced the Festival Tithe (or the Levitical Tithe) in years 3 and 6, but there are several problems with this view. First, how would the Israelites celebrate the festivals if they had no tithe by which to celebrate them? Second, how were the Levites supported if they were not given tithes? Regardless, even if the Charity Tithe replaced another tithe, the amount given per year was still not 10 percent.

Still the issue is even more complicated: the Israelites were only to give about 20 percent of the produce of the crops and cattle, but not all their income. While it is true that Israel was mainly an agricultural society, many Israelites had other professions and they did deal with money. Some Israelites were carpenters or fisherman: neither of these necessarily had any crops or cattle (though they could). The income one earned from being a fisherman, for example, was not subject to the laws of tithing in the Mosaic Law.

Furthermore, they did not give exactly 10 percent or 20 percent for the animal part of the tithe. Notice what Leviticus 27:32 says: "Every tenth animal from the herd or flock, which passes under the shepherd's rod, will be holy to the LORD" (HCSB). If an Israelite had ten animals, one would go toward his tithe: 10 percent. But, if he had twenty-two animals, two would go toward his tithe: about 9 percent. If an Israelite had nineteen animals, his "tithe" would actually equal about 5 percent! So what *percentage of income* did an Israelite actually give in order to obey the Mosaic Law on tithing? No one actually knows! The percentage would be different for everyone and they were only required to give from their crops and cattle.

There are several other aspects of giving in the Mosaic Law, the details of which are not overly pertinent to the current study. But there is a "sub-tithe" of the Levitical Tithe in Numbers 18 called the Priestly Tithe and there is a completely different tithe described in Amos 4:4. The precise definition of "offerings" is not too important, but nonetheless they do not refer to "rounding up" your tithe amount. In the end, some estimates say that Israelites gave between 30-50 percent of their increase from the land in contributions, which included the support of the religious system and the government.

CONCLUSION

Please keep in mind the biblical definition of the word tithe as you proceed in reading. Each section will open with a summary of the way tithing proponents argue for the Christian requirement to give 10 percent of one's income. That will be followed by a response to the argument. The sections are not ordered canonically, but in order of the strength of the argument: the weaker arguments will be presented at the beginning and the stronger arguments will presented later in the chapter. You may find some arguments silly and others compelling. You may disagree with the strength of the argument that the order indicates. Regardless, each argument deserves consideration and response, and that is what the bulk of this book intends to do.

Why spill so much effort in deconstructing the prevailing tithing paradigm? Christians find that giving 10 percent is so easy to calculate and, especially for many Americans, so easy to actually accomplish financially. It is tempting to conclude that as long as they are giving 10 percent, they can feel justified in doing whatever they want with the rest of their money and miss the opportunity to truly be blessed with a wise stewardship over their finances. My hope is that you will realize that giving 10 percent of your income cannot be defended biblically as a requirement. I want to aid you to construct a paradigm for giving completely independent from a 10 percent requirement. The final chapter will be the longest in this book and will hopefully be used to give guidance to the question: if not 10 percent, then what?!

2

OLD TESTAMENT ARGUMENTS
FOR TITHING

INTRODUCTION

There are several ways in which pro-tithing advocates have argued for tithing from the Old Testament. It is totally insufficient to respond to these arguments by saying that the Old Testament is irrelevant for Christians. At the very least, Paul didn't think the Old Testament was irrelevant, declaring that all Scripture is "profitable for teaching, for rebuking, for correcting, for training in righteousness" (2 Timothy 3:16, HCSB).[2] Therefore, it is incompatible with the teaching of the New Testament to brush aside these arguments; they need to be handled one by one.

ARGUMENT FROM THE GARDEN

God has always set aside a sacred portion for himself and the fact that he did this in the Garden of Eden by setting aside a portion of the trees demonstrates the universality of tithing.[3] According to

---

2 See Thomas D. Lea and Hayne P. Griffin, *1, 2 Timothy, Titus*, New American Commentary, vol. 34 (Nashville: Broadman & Holman Publishers, 2001), 235, who conclude that "Scripture" in this verse refers to the Old Testament.

3 This is a summary of the argument from John Albert May, *The Law of God on Tithes and Offerings or God's Plan to Finance His Church*, 3d ed, rev. and enl. (Nashville: M. E. Church, 1919), 7; Julius Earl Crawford, *The Call to Christian Stewardship* (Nashville: M. E. South, 1926), 15; Orval D. Peterson, *Stewardship in the Bible* (Bethany Study Course. St. Louis: Bethany, 1952), 25; Milo Kauffman, *The Challenge of Christian*

May, three institutions were instituted by God in the Garden of Eden: marriage, Sabbath, and tithing. All three are still applicable for Christians.[4] In fact, this argument can be traced back to the first command God ever gave to man, the command not to eat from the tree of the knowledge of good and evil. Adam and Eve sinned because they violated God's law in taking from the separated portion. This is what brought the "curse of God upon the human race."[5] The sin was serious because violating the separated portion was an attack on God as owner of the world. Some say that the specific percentage of trees separated wasn't explicitly stated in Scripture until Genesis 14, even though the principle should be traced back to the Garden. Others say that the specific percentage is unknown, but that it was a sacred portion. In the end, it is very difficult to understand the contents of Genesis unless God revealed to man the command to tithe.

One of the difficulties in refuting some of the arguments that advocate tithing is that they use arguments from silence.[6] These kinds of arguments aren't always weak, and, when crafted carefully, they can contain much merit.[7] Several issues need to be considered: (1) the relationship between Sabbath keeping and tithing; (2) the lack of any verbal hints regarding a separated/sacred portion of trees; and (3) the assertion that the sin that caused the Fall was violating the separated portion.

Stewardship (Scottdale, PA: Herald Press, 1955), 60; Morgan Cove, *An Essay on the Revenues of the Church of England: With An Inquiry into the Necessity, Justice, and Policy of an Abolition or Commutation of Tithes*, 3d. (London: F. C. and J. Rivington, 1816), 33.

4   May, *Law of God on Tithes*, 7.

5   Crawford, *Christian Stewardship*, 15.

6   The best example of this argument from silence is by Cove, who refers "to some unrecorded revelation made to Adam, and by him and his descendents [sic] delivered down to posterity" (Cove, *Essay on the Revenues*, 33).

7   See D. A. Carson, *Exegetical Fallacies*, 2d ed. (Grand Rapids: Baker, 1996), 138-39.

While the first of these issues will be addressed later,[8] issue (2) poses a serious problem for advocates of this argument. There is nothing in the text of Genesis 1-3 whatsoever that hints that there is an issue about a certain percentage or portion of trees being set aside. In fact, the language of Genesis 2:9b seems to imply that there was an abundance of trees in the Garden for Adam and Eve to enjoy: "every tree pleasing in appearance and good for food" (HCSB). Kenneth Matthews says, "Any charge that God is stingy is unfounded,"[9] and Sarna says that "The human couple will not be able to plead deprivation as the excuse for eating the forbidden fruit."[10] Therefore, this is an argument from silence that is unconvincing.

Issue (3) is difficult to assess since many theories have been proposed regarding the Fall.[11] The tree of the knowledge of good and evil appears to provide divine wisdom to those who eat of its fruit. While humans are encouraged to pursue wisdom (e.g., Proverbs 3:13), it is through fearing the Lord and not getting it apart from Him. The method Adam and Eve used to obtain wisdom, that is, through disobeying God's command, was a declaration of independence from God. By obtaining the wisdom in an unlawful manner, they sinned against God.

The Fall of mankind has nothing to do with tithing or a separated/sacred portion. The wording of Genesis 2 seems to imply that there were many trees in the Garden of Eden, not just ten. Therefore, the portion that God declared "off-limits" does not appear to be ten percent, but probably much less. The Fall was likely due to Adam and Eve declaring their independence by obtaining wisdom through disobedience, not violating a sacred portion.

---

8   See Chapter 4, Theological Arguments for Tithing, for a discussion on this.

9   Kenneth A. Mathews, *Genesis 1-11:26*, New American Commentary, vol. 1A (Nashville: Broadman & Holman Publishers, 2001), 201-02.

10 Nahum M. Sarna, *Genesis,* The JPS Torah Commentary (Philadelphia: Jewish Publication Society, 1989), 18.

11 For the following view, see Mathews, *Genesis 1-11:26*, 205-06.

TITHING AS THE ELEVENTH COMMANDMENT

Exodus 20:1-17 contains the Ten Commandments which were to be obeyed immediately by all of Israel. Leviticus 25-27 contains more commands given to Moses when he was on Mount Sinai (cf. Leviticus 25:1-2), but these were laws to be obeyed once they entered the land. Moses reviewed the Second and Fourth Commandments and applied them to the situation Israel would be in once they entered the land. To the Second and Fourth Commandment, an Eleventh Commandment is added. Since the command for the Israelites to tithe is placed within this context (i.e., Leviticus 27:30-33), it should be considered to be as binding as the rest of the Ten Commandments.[12]

There are several ways to approach this argument. One way would be to attack the assumption that the Ten Commandments are *de facto* still binding for Christians. While this might be a profitable discussion, it would lead the discussion away from a textual analysis. Furthermore, this issue is too large for this context and has been covered adequately in other arenas. Another approach would be to make some observations regarding the text of Leviticus 25-27 itself. This approach should provide an adequate response to this argument.

First, is Leviticus 25-27 really only applying the Second and Fourth Commandments to a new context and then adding on tithing? Not really. The first section (Leviticus 25:13ff.) gives details about how to keep the Year of Jubilee. Leviticus 26 begins with a restatement of the Second Commandment, but quickly moves into a discussion on the Mosaic Covenant in general, that is, rewards for obedience (Leviticus 26:3-13) and punishment for disobedience (Leviticus 26:14-45). This is not merely an application of two of the Ten Commandments.

---

12 John E. Simpson, *"He That Giveth:" A Study of the Stewardship of Money as Taught in Scripture* (New York: Revell, 1935), 54-55.

Second, Leviticus 27 is discussing the topic of special vows made to God: "Speak to the Israelites and tell them: When someone makes a special vow to the LORD that involves the assessment of people" (Leviticus 27:2, HCSB). Chapter 27 then discusses laws on "vows," which are not a part of the Second or Fourth Commandments. Moreover, Leviticus 27:26 shifts to discuss items that are *not* subject to vows, namely, the firstlings of animals, any devoted thing, and the tithe of the land.

Finally, if tithing is required for the reasons stated above, then all the laws stated in these sections are equally applicable: all the laws about the Year of Jubilee, about rewards and punishments in the Mosaic Covenant, and about vows. The discussion on tithing in Leviticus 27 is not connected directly or indirectly to the Ten Commandments.

ARGUMENT FROM ABEL'S OFFERING

The reason that Abel's offering was accepted, while Cain's was rejected, is because Abel tithed and Cain did not. Two avenues can be explored in support of this contention.[13] First, some interpret-

13 S. B. Shaw, *God's Financial Plan or Temporal Prosperity: The Result of Faithful Stewardship* (Chicago: Shaw, 1897), 42-43; [Kenrick Peck], *The Universal Obligation of Tithes* (London: Elliot Stock, 1901), 85-92; E. B. Stewart, *The Tithe* (Chicago: Winona Publishing, 1903), 37; Henry Lansdell, *The Sacred Tenth or Studies in Tithe-Giving Ancient and Modern*, 2 vols. (1906. Reprint, 2 vols. In 1, Grand Rapids: Baker, 1955), 41-42; John Wesley Duncan, *Our Christian Stewardship* (New York: Eaton & Mains, 1909), 44; Arthur V. Babbs, *The Law of the Tithe: As Set Forth in the Old Testament* (New York: Revell, 1912), 25; May, *Law of God on Tithes*, 11; P. W. Thompson, *The Whole Tithe* (London: Marshall Brothers, [1920]), 11; Crawford, *Christian Stewardship*, 15-16; Simpson, *Stewardship of Money*, 52; Oscar Lowry, *Should Christians Tithe?* (Fort Wayne: Glad Tidings, [1940s]), 7; George A. E. Salstrand, *The Tithe: The Minimum Standard for Christian Giving* (Grand Rapids: Baker, 1952), 19-21; Merrill D. Moore, *Found Faithful: Christian Stewardship in Personal and Church Life* (Nashville: Broadman, 1953), 22; Kauffman, *Challenge*, 60; Charley Holmes, "Tithing: A Timeless Moral Imperative or Old Testa-

ers have understood the way the Septuagint (LXX) translated the Hebrew Old Testament as a reference to tithing. The LXX suggests that Cain's sacrifice was not acceptable to God because he did not "divide rightly." The word used in the LXX is *diaireō,* which means "I distribute, divide." Those who advocate this view need to justify why they accept the LXX translation and ignore the Hebrew text at this point. The Hebrew refers to "not doing well" rather than "not dividing rightly." Furthermore, the assertion that "dividing" refers to a certain percentage being given to God is an assumption. This same word is used in the Pentateuch ten more times, never in the context of tithing,[14] and in the cultic context of Leviticus, it appears to refer to "cutting." In fact, Thayer's lexicon includes "to tear, cleave or cut asunder" as part of the definition.[15] Finally, it is most likely that the translators of the LXX misunderstood the Hebrew word *seeth* ("to lift up") in reference to raising a sacrifice. While it can mean that, it can also refer to lifting up one's face or countenance (referring to a sign of favor). It appears that they confused *seeth* with *rum,* which is a reference to lifting sacrifices.

Second, some tithing advocates utilize Genesis 4:7 to argue for a pre-Abrahamic tithe by comparing it to Hebrews 11:4. Some scholars believe that Abel's sacrifice is described as more abundant than Cain's sacrifice. The Greek word, *polus,* can refer to quality, quantity, or something being more appropriate. The word is used three other times in Hebrews: 3:3 (twice) and 7:23. The latter verse clearly refers to the priests being more numerous, or, larger in quantity. However, Hebrews 3:3 says, "For Jesus is considered worthy of more glory than Moses, just as the builder has more honor than the house" (HCSB). The "more" in this verse does not appear to refer to quantity. The context of Hebrews 11:4 is a little

---

ment Legalism?" (D.Min. dissertation, Reformed Theological Seminary, 1998), 33-37.

14 The word is also used in Genesis 15:10 (twice); 32:8; Exodus 21:35; Leviticus 1:12, 17; 5:8; Numbers 31:27, 42.

15 Joseph Henry Thayer, *A Greek-English Lexicon of the New Testament* (New York: American Book Company, 1889), 137.

helpful, based upon the context being faith. This would appear to favor the qualitative aspect. Most of the major translations favor this reading as well (cf. ESV, NASB, HCSB, NIV, NKJV, NLT).

ARGUMENT FROM MALACHI 3

One of the most well-known and oft-used arguments for the continuation of tithing is Malachi 3:6-12. Since Malachi 3 declares that withholding tithes is equivalent to robbing God, Christians should tithe. Malachi warns followers of God that withholding the paying of your tithe today will bring the curses mentioned in Malachi 3. Sometimes proponents of the Malachi 3 argument relate the withholding of tithes to the commandment against stealing.[16]

Malachi 3:6 begins with a shift in the audience: rather than just addressing the priests, God is now addressing all of Israel. Which tithe is Malachi 3 discussing? Most likely he has in mind the Levitical Tithe of Numbers 18:21, not the Festival Tithe of Deuteronomy 14:22-27, nor the Charity Tithe of Deuteronomy 14:28-29. The Festival Tithe was to be brought to Jerusalem and the people were to celebrate with the priests. Since the people were partakers in the feast, the tithe still belonged to the people. In contrast, the tithe in Malachi 3 was brought into the "storehouse," which seems to be a reference to the Levitical Tithe since that was to be brought to Jerusalem.

God told the people that they were robbing him of "tithes and offerings." The tithe that was meant for the support of the

---

16 Jerome (cited by John Sharp, "Tithes," in *Dictionary of Christian Antiquities,* 2 vols., ed. William Smith and Samuel Cheetham [London: John Murray, 1893], 2:1964); George D. Watson, *Soul Food: Being Chapters on the Interior Life with Passages of Personal Experience* (Cincinnati: Knapp, 1896), 98; Frank H. Leavell, *Training in Stewardship* (Nashville: Sunday School Board Southern Baptist Convention, 1920), 64; Stephen Olford, *The Grace of Giving: Thoughts on Financial Stewardship* (Grand Rapids: Zondervan, 1972), 28-29; Larry Burkett, *Giving and Tithing* (Chicago: Moody, 1991), 36; William D. Watley, *Bring the Full Tithe: Sermons on the Grace of Giving* (Valley Forge: Judson, 1995), 7.

Levites and priests was not being given as commanded in the Law. The term "offerings" is often misunderstood, but it also referred to required contributions. These were used for the support of the temple staff.

The reference to the "storehouse" is another important aspect of this passage. The storehouse did not refer to "local churches," but an actual building used by the Levites that they used to store what they received, including grains and livestock. 2 Chronicles 31:10-12 references the storehouse, but it was not necessarily part of the Mosaic Law; it was built onto the temple for storage purposes. That is what makes correlating the "storehouse" to "local churches" so problematic.

Several preachers have made deals with their congregations: start tithing and if God doesn't bless you after a certain time period (sometimes three months, sometimes six months), the church will refund the money. This is based upon the offer to "test" God in Malachi 3. It's important to note at least the following two points. First, this offer to test God occurs in the context of the Mosaic Covenant. The blessings and curses of Deuteronomy 28 are in full effect during Malachi 3. Second, the offer to test God is modified by "in this" (cf. NASB). The phrase "in this" refers to testing God in the current situation, not necessarily to test Him in all periods at all times.[17]

The rewards for Israelite obedience in giving their tithes and offerings were threefold. First, God would open the windows of heaven. This is a promise of rain. Second, God would prevent the devourer from ruining their crops. The devourer is a reference to locusts. Third, God would stop their vines from casting their fruit; rather they would have abundant crops. Some scholars have said that agrarian blessings are offered because they lived in an agrarian society. While it is true that Israel was largely agrarian, they were not *purely* an agricultural society. They did deal in money and had other industries.

---

17 The phrase "in this" could also refer to "in this matter," that is, the matter of tithing. Cf. NET.

Malachi 3 was written to an audience (the Israelites) that was under the Mosaic Covenant and was therefore subject to the stipulations of that covenant (cf. Deuteronomy 28). The test was not stated in universal terms, but very specific terms. The Israelites were failing to pay the Levitical Tithe, which was required for the support of the Levites since they did not get an inheritance of land in Israel. The promised reward does not *de facto* carry over for New Covenant believers. The exact amount of an offering is perplexing, but it was just as required as the tithe. The offering was not a certain monetary amount, making it virtually non-transferable for believers in the New Covenant.

ARGUMENT FROM THE MOSAIC LAW

The argument from the Mosaic Law begins with Deuteronomy 16:17: "Everyone must appear with a gift suited to his means, according to the blessing the LORD your God has given you" (HCSB). Paul was referencing this Old Testament text in 1 Corinthians 16:2: "On the first day of the week, each of you is to set something aside and save in keeping with how he prospers, so that no collections will need to be made when I come" (HCSB). Since Paul was alluding to this text in the Mosaic Law, tithing, which was the prescribed proportion in the Law, is still binding on Christians.[18]

Deuteronomy 16:16-17 is a summary of the entire section of 14:22-16:17. Though the three festivals had different origins and purposes, they were all occasions for Israelites to worship God through giving. The section begins with a direct reference to tithing (Deuteronomy 14:22) and ends with a veiled reference. However, how clearly is this a parallel to 1 Corinthians 16:2?

First, the lack of specific verbal parallels between the LXX of Deuteronomy 16:17 and the Greek of 1 Corinthians 16:2 is strik-

18 William Speer, *God's Rule for Christian Giving: A Practical Essay on the Science of Christian Economy* (Philadelphia: Presbyterian Board of Publication, 1875), 106-13; 244-58; A. J. Gordon, *God's Tenth* (Richmond: Foreign Mission Board, Southern Baptist Convention, [1880s]), 2-3.

ing. There are hardly any words that match, though the concepts are similar.

Parallels between Deuteronomy 16:16-17 and 1 Corinthians 16:2

	Deuteronomy 16:16-17	**1 Corinthians 16:2**
When	Three times per year	First day of every week
Who	Every man	Each one of you
What	Give	Put aside and save
How much	As he is able; According to the blessing	As he may prosper
Source	Of the LORD your God	Divine passive[19]

This is not enough of a parallel to say that Paul is advocating tithing in 1 Corinthians 16:2. In fact, some of the differences (such as the "when" category) are significant. Furthermore, as will be explained in the following chapter, relating 1 Corinthians 16 to tithing is problematic. Even if Paul were alluding to Deuteronomy 16:17, that would not necessitate that he was commanding the tithe for Christians. It is one thing to advocate giving to God; it is another to assume a specific amount is required.

ARGUMENT FROM ABRAHAM

Some tithing proponents believe that tithing is binding upon Christians because it was practiced before the Mosaic Law was given, extending back at least to Abram. Genesis 14:20 references Abram[20] giving Melchizedek "a tenth of everything." If tithing extends into the period before the Mosaic Law, then it must not be

---

19 The Greek has an awkward phrase: "whatever has been prospered." The verb is in the passive voice, most likely indicating that God is the one who has prospered them.
20 This occurs before his name was changed to Abraham.

tied to the Mosaic Law. Therefore, tithing would be binding upon all Christians.[21]

In response, the underlying assumption to this argument is that Abram's tithe and the tithe described in the Mosaic Law are the same. There are at least six differences between the two. First, Abram's tithe was connected to a vow he had made *before* he went to war. The vow was that he would not keep any of the war booty. So 10 percent was given to Melchizedek and the rest was given away. Abram gave away 100 percent of the war booty because of a vow, not 10 percent. The Mosaic Law strictly forbids any connection between tithing and vows (see Leviticus 27:30-33). Second, Abram is described as giving a tithe one time in his life; the Mosaic Law describes tithing as a consistent, systematic practice. If Abram tithed consistently, it is unknown to whom he would have given his tithe. Third, Abram's tithe was given to a priest named Melchizedek. Tithing in the Mosaic Law was (partially) for the Levites, a completely different line of priests from Melchizedek. Fourth, Abram voluntarily gave his tithe. Tithing is mandatory under the Mosaic Law. Fifth, Abram did not give the tithe from his possessions, but from the war booty (cf. Hebrews 7:4). Tithing in the Mosaic Law was from the increase of possessions connected to the land of Israel: crops and cattle. Also, the Mosaic Law did prescribe a mandatory giving from war booty: one out of every five hundred of the spoils (Numbers 31:27-29). Sixth, Abraham gave 10 percent to Melchizedek. Because of the multiple tithes described in the Mosaic Law, tithing was at least 20 percent per year for Israelites.

CONCLUSION

Six arguments for the continuation of tithing have been considered from the Old Testament in order of least convincing to most convincing. All of the arguments have significant issues that

---

21 Ken Hemphill and Bobby Eklund, "Foundations for Giving," in *Perspectives on Tithing: 4 Views,* ed. David A. Croteau (Nashville: Broadman & Holman, 2011), 27-28.

render them at least inconclusive and sometimes implausible. There is no evidence that the portion of trees withheld from Adam and Eve is close to 10 percent. Tithing should not be considered as the "Eleventh Commandment." It is unjustified to favor the LXX's reading over the Hebrew in order to find a reference to tithing in Abel's offering. Malachi 3, while a popular passage to use, is problematic as a basis for storehouse tithing for several reasons. Paul was not directly alluding to the practice of tithing in his epistles. While Abraham's encounter with Melchizedek is the strongest argument from the Old Testament, there were still several problems with utilizing it for the continuation of tithing. However, several arguments remain from the New Testament, which will be considered next.

3

NEW TESTAMENT ARGUMENTS FOR TITHING

INTRODUCTION

While the Old Testament did not contain any arguments convincingly demonstrating that the command for tithing continues into the New Covenant, six additional arguments from the New Testament are utilized by tithing proponents. The New Testament is the final authority for faith and practice for Christians. If the New Testament contains a command for Christians to tithe, then Christians must tithe. The arguments below include passages from the Gospels, Paul's first letter to the Corinthians, and the Epistle to the Hebrews.

ARGUMENT FROM JESUS' EXAMPLE

Jesus was never accused of failing to tithe. Pharisees would resist eating with a law-breaker, including someone who did not tithe. Since the Pharisees ate with Jesus, this demonstrates that he was not a law breaker on tithing. Since Jesus tithed, so should Christians.[22]

---

22 Lansdell, *Sacred Tenth*, 137-45, 157; Duncan, *Christian Stewardship*, 53-56; Simpson, *Stewardship of Money*, 59; W. L. Muncy, Jr., *Fellowship with God through Christian Stewardship* (Kansas City: Central Seminary Press, 1949), 131; J. E. Dillard, *Good Stewards* (Nashville: Broadman, 1953), 86-87; Herschel H. Hobbs, *The Gospel of Giving* (Nashville: Broadman, 1954), 17; Kauffman, *Challenge*, 68; Robert J. Hastings, *My Money and God* (Nashville: Broadman, 1961), 63; Fletcher Clarke Spruce, *You Can Be a Joyful Tither* (Kansas City: Beacon Hill, 1966), 20; W. E. Grindstaff, *Principles of Stewardship Development* (Nashville: Convention Press, 1967), 20; H. Franklin Paschall, "Tithing in the New

It is true that Jesus was never accused of being a law-breaker where tithing is concerned. However, certain aspects of the definition of tithing under the Mosaic Law must be remembered: first, the tithe was at least 20 percent per year; and second, it only applied to the increase in crops and cattle.

First, if Jesus tithed, it needs to be remembered that he paid about 20 percent yearly in tithes, not 10 percent. If this argument holds, then Christians today must also pay about 20 percent every year, not just 10 percent.

Second, Jesus would only be required to pay tithes on crops and cattle. What was Jesus' profession? Jesus was a builder, one who worked with wood and stones in construction.[23] This means that he did not primarily work in agriculture, with crops or cattle. Therefore, any income Jesus received from construction projects would not be subject to tithing. Several professions did not have to pay tithes on their income, including artisans, fishermen, and tradesmen; priests and the poor (those who did not own land nor animals) were exempt from tithes.[24]

Therefore, Pharisees would have eaten with someone of Jesus' profession without worrying about his practice of tithing since he would not have typically been involved in tithing. The absence of an accusation against Jesus is irrelevant.

Testament," in *Resource Unlimited*, ed. William L. Hendricks (Nashville: Stewardship Commission of the Southern Baptist Convention, 1972), 169-171; Samuel Young, *Giving and Living: Foundations for Christian Stewardship* (1974. Reprint, Grand Rapids: Baker, 1976), 26; Robert T. Kendall, *Tithing: A Call to Serious, Biblical Giving* (Grand Rapids: Zondervan, 1982), 29; Randy Alcorn, *Money, Possessions, and Eternity* (Wheaton: Tyndale, 1989), 214-15.

23 See Ken M. Campbell, "What Was Jesus' Occupation?" *Journal of the Evangelical Theological Society* 48:3 (2005): 502-19.

24 See Frederick C. Grant, *The Economic Background of the Gospels* (London: Oxford, 1926), 95, n. 1.

THE CAESARIAN ARGUMENT

In Matthew 22:15-22, Jesus is confronted with a "trick question" about paying taxes by the disciples of the Pharisees. He responds by telling them to give to Caesar the things which are Caesar's and to give to God the things that are God's. Caesar was due taxes, so Christians should pay their taxes. God is due tithes, so Christians should pay tithes.[25]

The main question from this text is: does the phrase "the things that are God's" refer to tithing? The two other times that phrase is used in the New Testament (Matthew 16:23 and 1 Corinthians 2:11) the context makes clear the referent (God's interests and the thoughts of God). The current context is quite ambiguous. The only hint that it could refer to tithing is the understanding that the Greek verb translated "give" (*apodidōmi*) means "to give back" or "return." However, it makes little sense to understand that verb to mean that in this context since paying taxes to Caesar was not "giving back."[26] Therefore, the main point of this text in the context of Matthew's Gospel should reign: <u>Christians should not turn away from their obligations to God while still rendering to Caesar what belongs to Caesar.</u>

ARGUMENT FROM HEBREWS

Hebrews 7 proves that Christians should tithe. It explains that Abraham paid tithes to Melchizedek. Since tithes were due to Melchizedek, and Jesus is in the line of Melchizedek, tithes are now due to Jesus. Verse 8 explicitly declares this by saying that previously

---

25 John Gough, *Tracts on Tithes* (Dublin: Jackson, 1786), contained three tracts. The second, "Plain Reasons why the People called Quakers may in Conscience, and ought in Duty, to pay Tithes," published in 1786, was said to be written by a Prelate of the Kingdom. See the second tract, 18-22. See also Kauffman, *Christian Stewardship*, 68; Gary DeMar, *God and Government: Issues in Biblical Perspective, vol. 2* (Brentwood, TN: Wolgemuth & Hyatt, 1989), 113.
26 Contra HCSB.

"mortal men" received tithes, but now "one *receives them,* of whom it is witnessed that he lives on" (NASB). Also, while Melchizedek is a picture of Christ, Abraham is a picture of Christians today who should pay their tithes to Christ.[27]

The literary argument of Hebrews as a whole, and of this passage in particular, is important to consider. The entire letter to the Hebrews is basically arguing that Jesus' sacrifice is superior to the Old Covenant sacrifices; therefore, the Jews were encouraged not to turn back to their former ways. The author goes through many steps to prove the superiority of Jesus' sacrifice. He demonstrates Jesus' superiority to the angels and then the superiority of Jesus' high priesthood to Aaron's priesthood. Then the author proves that Melchizedek's priesthood was superior to the Levitical priesthood. Then, on the basis of Psalm 110:4, the author shows that Jesus' priesthood and Melchizedek's priesthood were of the same kind. Since Melchizedek's priesthood was just proved to be superior to the Levitical priesthood, Jesus's priesthood is also superior to the Levitical priesthood. The section of Hebrews 7:1-10 is attempting to prove that Melchizedek's priesthood is greater than the Levitical priesthood.

The first three verses of Hebrews 7:1-10 have one major theme: Melchizedek remains a priest forever. This text is not about a pre-incarnation appearance of Jesus or whether Melchizedek is Jesus. In verse 4 there is a shift to the next phase of the argument, the

27 Babbs, *Law of the Tithe,* 217; Leavell, *Training,* 67; Simpson, *Stewardship of Money,* 60; Muncy, *Fellowship,* 132-33; Moore, *Found Faithful,* 42; Jarrette Aycock, *Tithing-Your Questions Answer* (Kansas City: Beacon Hill, 1955), 12; Kauffman, *Challenge,* 71; Luther P. Powell, *Money and the Church* (New York: Association Press, 1962), 223; Spruce, *Joyful Tither,* 21; W. W. Barndollar, "Scriptural Tithe" (Th.D. diss., Grace Theological Seminary, 1959), 201-03; Arthur W. Pink, *Tithing* (Swengel, PA: Reiner, 1967), 16; Olford, *Grace of Giving,* 30; Brooks H. Wester, "The Christian and the Tithe," in *Classic Sermons on Stewardship,* compiled by Warren W. Wiersbe, Kregel Classic Sermons (Grand Rapids: Kregel, 1999), 160; John J. Mitchell, "Tithing, Yes!" *Presbyterian Guardian* 47 (October 1978): 6.

"proofs." Three reasons are provided to support the contention that Melchizedek's priesthood was greater than the Levitical priesthood. First, Melchizedek is greater than Abraham because he received tithes from Abraham. Since Levi and Aaron were both descended from Abraham, Melchizedek's superiority to them is proven. Second, Melchizedek blessed Abraham, and the greater always blesses the lesser. Third, Levitical priests would begin their service in the Temple at a certain age and then they would cease serving. They would eventually die. Israel paid tithes to priests who would die, but Abraham paid his tithes to a priest who lives on: Melchizedek.

This last point is significant because verse 8 is talking about Melchizedek, not Jesus.[28] Verse 8 does not declare that Jesus receives tithes, but the contrast is specifically between Aaronic priests who received tithes and died versus Melchizedek who received tithes but did not die. Hebrews 7:3 says that Melchizedek has "neither beginning of days nor end of life" and that "he remains a priest perpetually" (NASB). The author only turns his attention to Christ in verse 11 and following.

Also, is Abraham a picture of Christians giving tithes today? If Abraham was intended to be a picture of Christians paying tithes today, what about the inconsistencies between his act of tithing and what is taught today? First, Abraham's tithe was voluntary, not compulsory. Scripture never declares that he was required to give a tithe or that he was commanded to give it. Second, his tithe was given as a thanksgiving to God for his victory in war. This is very different from the picture of tithing in the Mosaic Law. Finally, the main objection, the author of Hebrews was not attempting to argue for a continuation of the practice of tithing in this passage. The issue of the continuation or cessation of tithing is totally irrelevant to the author's theological purposes in Hebrews. The reference to tithing in Hebrews 7 is illustrative, not prescriptive. Ellingworth's

---

28 Note that the words "receives them" and "he" in verse 8 are not in the Greek text but are provided in the NASB translation for clarity.

conclusion is judicious: "Abraham's action is unrelated to the later Mosaic legislation on tithes ... and this is not Hebrews' concern."[29]

ARGUMENT FROM JESUS' TEACHING

Matthew 23:23 and Luke 11:42 should be understood as Jesus commanding Christians to tithe. Rather than referring to Matthew 23:23 as a command, some use commend, endorse, approve, or sanction. Furthermore, if Jesus wanted to abrogate the law, this was the perfect time to do that.[30]

There are three main points to consider when utilizing Matthew 23:23 to argue for the continuation of tithing. First, Jesus was speaking to Jews in Matthew 23 who were living under the Old Covenant. Of course Jesus "commended" them for tithing; Old Covenant Jews were required to tithe. He would have commended them for circumcising their children or for keeping the year of Jubilee or for obeying the Levirate Law (see Genesis 38; Deuteronomy 25:5-10; Ruth 4; and Matthew 22:23-28). Commending

---

29 Paul Ellingworth, *The Epistle to the Hebrews: A Commentary on the Greek Text*, NIGTC (Grand Rapids: Eerdmans, 1993), 361.

30 Hilary, *Commentary on Matthew 23* (cited by Thomas J. Powers, "An Historical Study of the Tithe in the Christian Church to 1648" (Ph.D. diss., Southern Baptist Theological Seminary, 1948), 42; Lansdell, *Sacred Tenth*, 192-93; A. T. Robertson, *Five Times Five Points of Church Finance*, 2d ed. (Lima: n.p., 1886), 124; Stewart, *Tithe*, 62; Duncan, *Christian Stewardship*, 16, 53-56; Leavell, *Training*, 19; James A. Hensey, *Storehouse Tithing or Stewardship-Up-To-Date* (New York: Revell, 1922), 40-41; Luther E. Lovejoy, *Stewardship for All of Life, Life and Service Series* (New York: Methodist Book Concern, 1924), 98; Lowry, *Should Christians*, 8; Salstrand, *Tithe*, 31; Costen J. Harrell, *Stewardship and the Tithe* (New York: Abingdon, 1953), 46; John R. Rice, *All about Christian Giving* (Wheaton: Sword of the Lord, 1954), 27-28; Aycock, *Tithing*, 11-12; Richard V. Clearwaters, *Stewardship Sermonettes* (Grand Rapids: Baker, 1955), 25-26; Kauffman, *Challenge*, 67; Pink, *Tithing*, 12; Olford, *Grace of Giving*, 31; Paschall, "Tithing," 171; Holmes, "Tithing," 85; Barndollar, "Scriptural Tithe," 159; Hank Hanegraaff, *The Bible Answer Book* (Nashville: J. Countryman, 2004), 75.

Old Covenant saints for keeping the Old Covenant Law does not mean that Christians must keep those laws. As New Testament scholar Craig Blomberg concludes: "The last sentence of v. 23 does not imply … that tithing is mandated of Christians, merely that as long as the Mosaic Covenant remains in force (up to the time of Jesus' death and resurrection), all of it must be obeyed but with discernment of its true priorities."[31]

Second, there is debate over whether or not Jews had to tithe "mint and dill and cummin" (or, "mint and rue and every kind of garden herb" as in Luke 11:42). In the Mishnah, Maaserot 4:5, a debate occurred over the tithing of coriander and dill. In-stone-Brewer analyzes the debate and concludes that it reaches back before 70 A.D.[32] Rabbi Eliezer ben Hyrcanus (ca. 40-120 A.D.) said that dill needed to be tithed.[33] However, Shebiit 9:1 declared that other small plants, including rue, were exempt from the laws of tithing. This is important so that it can be known what exactly Jesus is "commending": was it faithfulness to the Old Testament Law or to Jewish oral traditions? The answer is probably found in the parallel in Luke 11:42: "and every kind of garden herb." It is clear that it was not necessary to tithe every herb.[34] Therefore, Jesus is simply commending the Jews for their meticulousness in tithing. This means that he is not explicitly commending obedience to a specific Old Testament Law or practice, but to a contemporary manifestation of that practice.

---

31 Craig Blomberg, *Matthew*, New American Commentary, vol. 22 (Nashville: Broadman & Holman Publishers, 2001), 346.

32 David Instone-Brewer, *Prayer and Agriculture, Traditions of Rabbis from the Era of the New Testament,* vol.1 (Grand Rapids: Eerdmans, 2004), 314-17.

33 Maaserot 4:5. This rabbi received significant praise for his decisions and faithfulness to tradition (see Instone-Brewer, *Prayer and Agriculture*, 28).

34 See Robert H. Stein, *Luke,* New American Commentary, vol. 24 (Nashville: Broadman & Holman, 2001), 341, and Leon Morris, *The Gospel According to Matthew* (Grand Rapids: Eerdmans, 1992), 582.

Third, if Jesus was commending the Old Testament practice, then he was commending a 23 percent tithe, specifically on crops from the ground and cattle. However, if Jesus was commending the contemporary manifestation of the Old Testament Laws, then he was commending either a 20 percent or 23 percent tithe on crops and cattle only. Either way, this is not what contemporary advocates of tithing claim as Jesus' commendation: 10 percent of income.

Jesus was surely commending the Jews of his time for their practice. This does not automatically mean that he was "commanding" Christians to do the same. Whatever the specifics of the commendation in Matthew 23:23 (and Luke 11:42), it was not a commendation to give 10 percent of income. If contemporary tithing advocates want to use these texts to advance their argument, they will need to adjust their definition of tithing away from 10 percent of income.

TITHING IS FROM ALL INCOME

In Luke 18:9, Jesus begins telling a parable about a tax collector and a Pharisee. The Pharisee prays and declares that he gives "a tenth of everything I get" (Luke 18:12, HCSB). Even though this is a parable, it demonstrates that the Jews did not just tithe from produce of the land, but from any source of income they had. Therefore, tithing is easily transferable to contemporary Christianity and Christians must give a tithe from all their income.

The Pharisee certainly declared that he tithed.[35] He also stated that he paid his tithe from all that he got, a verb that refers to gaining possession or acquiring (cf. Matthew 10:9; Acts 8:20). However, it is at this point that paying careful attention to context, both literary and historical, can be beneficial.

In the literary context, the Pharisee also stated that he fasted twice per week. Fasting was only required on the Day of Atonement, according to the Old Testament (Leviticus 16:29-31). There

---

35 The use of the present tense would be consistent with the concept that he tithed on a consistent or continual basis.

was nothing wrong with fasting more often than this (if done with the right intentions), but fasting more often was *not* required. In the *Didache* (8:1), there is a reference to Jews fasting on Mondays and Thursdays. So the Pharisee was stating in his prayer that he went beyond what was required in the area of fasting.

When applied to tithing, the parallel should be evident. Jews were only required to tithe from the produce of the land and cattle, but this Pharisee went beyond that. Luke 11:42 also presents the Pharisees as being concerned about the minutiae. The problem in Luke 11 is that while they were overly concerned about small things, they were unconcerned with significant things. But why did the Pharisee give from all he acquired in Luke 18? This is where the historical context becomes important.

In the Mishnah there is a tractate called Demai. It explains that when Jews were unsure about whether or not something they were given or acquired needed to be tithed, the laws of Demai told them to "tithe" one percent. Therefore, when the Pharisee explains that he paid tithes on all that he acquired, he is declaring his obedience to the rules of Demai. Like fasting, this was going above and beyond what was required under the Old Testament Law and was a reference to the Oral Law.[36]

PAUL COMMENDED TITHING CONCEPTUALLY

The Apostle Paul never mentioned tithing explicitly. However, the concept is present in his epistles, especially 1 Corinthians 9:13-14 and 16:2. In the former he states that ministers of the gospel should be supported in the same way that the Levites and priests were supported: through tithes and offerings. In the latter he refers

---

36 Commenting on Luke 18:12, Stein says that the Pharisee "may have done this in case the person who sold this to him had not tithed it" (Stein, *Luke,* 449-50). It sounds like Stein may be referring to the Demai tithe of the Mishnah.

to giving as one has been prospered, or proportionately, which is a reference to tithing.[37]

Analyzing the context of 1 Corinthians 9 will provide sufficient data by which the argument by modern tithing advocates will be undone. 1 Corinthians 9 does not stand alone, but is directly connected to the preceding chapter. In 1 Corinthians 8, Paul is discussing the issue of food sacrificed to idols. His conclusion is that there is nothing inherently wrong with eating food that has been sacrificed to an idol, but he is willing to abdicate the right he has for the sake of other believers in Christ. Paul wants to provide an illustration of the concept of having a right, but putting love before *rights*. His illustration is about the financial support of preachers of the gospel.

This is how 1 Corinthians 9 fits into the context: it is an illustration of the concept of forsaking one's rights because of love for brothers and sisters in Christ. Paul gives several compelling arguments from nature for why preachers of the gospel should be supported: first, soldiers do not serve at their own expense; second, farmers eat some of the crops that they plant; and third, shepherds drink some of the milk from their flocks. Paul then gives two arguments from the Old Testament and one from the teaching of Jesus.

The first argument from the Old Testament is a quote from Deuteronomy 25:4 about oxen being allowed to eat while treading out grain. The second argument from the Old Testament is the

---

37 [Thomas Kane], "What We Owe and Why We Owe It," in *Tithing and Its Results* (Chicago: The Layman Company, 1915); Shaw, *Financial Plan,* 181; Charles A. Cook, *Systematic Giving: The Church's Safeguard against Nineteenth Century Evils* (Philadelphia: American Baptist Publication Society, 1903), 65-66; Stewart, *Tithe,* 62; Lansdell, *Sacred Tenth,* 170-71; May, *Law of God on Tithes,* 24; Leavell, *Training,* 64; Simpson, *Stewardship of Money,* 60; John D. Freeman, *More Than Money* (Nashville: Sunday School Board of the Southern Baptist Convention, 1935), 123; Salstrand, *Tithe,* 38; Hobbs, *Gospel of Giving,* 42-45; Aycock, *Tithing,* 12; Kauffman, *Challenge,* 65; Barndollar, "Scriptural Tithe," 170-71; Pink, *Tithing,* 13-14; Olford, *Grace of Giving,* 31; Mitchell, "Tithing," 7; Kendall, *Tithing,* 32.

key one for the concerns of tithing advocates: "Don't you know that those who perform the temple services eat the food from the temple, and those who serve at the altar share in the offerings of the altar" (1 Corinthians 9:13, HCSB)? This appears to be a clear reference to the support of the priests who served in the temple, which was commanded in the Mosaic Law. Ministers of God have the right to be supported for their spiritual service. Now notice how Paul connects verses 13 and 14: "so also" (NASB) or "in the same way" (HCSB, ESV). This phrase occurs ten times in 1 Corinthians (2:11; 9:14; 11:12; 12:12; 14:9, 12, 42, 45; 16:1) and it refers to a relationship, a correspondence, between two things, with the relationship typically referring to one point of correspondence between the two things. Can this phrase support the contention that it refers to tithes and offerings?

One way in which this argument could be made would be to say that while priests lived off the sacrificial system by means of the tithes and offerings given to them, preachers are to "earn their living by the gospel" (1 Corinthians 9:14, HCSB). In response to this argument, two questions arise: what is the relationship between the gospel and "tithes and offerings?" Also, can tithes and offerings be separated from the rest of the sacrificial system and applied to the gospel ministry?

The Mosaic Law sacrificial system pointed to the gospel. Lenski commented on this verse and said: "Christianity has superseded the old Temple ritual. Paul does not need to explain this change."[38] Mosaic Law sacrifices are no longer necessary because Christ became the once-for-all sacrifice. Therefore, appropriating "tithes and offerings" from the Mosaic Law appears inappropriate.

A second argument could be made from these verses: Paul, in verses 13-14, was saying that the ministry of preaching the gospel has replaced the ministry of the priests. Since the priests are no longer active, preachers of the gospel should receive the tithes that formerly went to the priests.

---

38 R. C. H. Lenski, *The Interpretation of St. Paul's First and Second Epistle to the Corinthians* (Columbus: Wartburg, 1946), 367.

In response, to utilize this argument consistently, the tithing advocate would have to view Paul, in some way, as a soldier, a farmer, a shepherd, and an ox. While some of these could be understood both literally (flock = flock of animals) or metaphorically (flock = followers of Christ), it does not work for all of them. Nowhere does Paul refer to himself analogously as an ox or any animal similar to it. Nothing in the context indicates that Paul is using a double entendre.

There are three other points in response to any kind of use of this passage for the requirement of Christians to tithe. First, priests did not get 10 percent of the income of Israelites. Priests received 10 percent of 10 percent (or, 1 percent) of the increase in crops and cattle at an average rate of at least 20 percent. If someone wants to interpret the phrase "in the same way" very literally or strictly, then this percentage would be the referent. Second, since the context is about having a right to something, but also having the ability to forgo utilizing that right, then a consistent application would be that Christians only need to give their tithes and offerings (which were never 10 percent of income) if the preacher decides to utilize their right. Third, the Gentile practice of tithing was radically different from the Jewish practice. If Paul is going to incorporate the Mosaic Law of tithing into the New Covenant, an explanation on how this would transfer over would be necessary, especially for Gentiles.

CONCLUSION

Six arguments from the New Testament have been considered. It is never stated that Jesus either did or did not tithe, but the paying of tithes under the Mosaic Law was limited to landowners who had crops and/or cattle. Craftsmen were exempt from paying tithes. The phrase "give to God that which is God's" is too ambiguous to be a clear reference to tithing. When the argument of the book of Hebrews is taken into consideration, utilizing Hebrews 7 to advocate the requirement of the tithe for Christians becomes problematic. While Jesus never commanded the cessation of tithing, his commendation in Matthew 23:23 does not adequately support the contention that Christians must tithe. The parable in Luke 18 cannot support the notion that tithing was supposed to be from all income. Finally, Paul's reference to those who served in the temple and at the altar, while the best argument for tithing in the New Testament, has several problematic aspects when the context of 1 Corinthians 8 is considered and when the practice of tithing from the Mosaic Law is remembered. If tithing is required for Christians, then arguments will need to be found outside the specific texts discussed above in the Old and New Testaments. Some tithing advocates find their basis in theological categories, rather than specific textual categories. These arguments will be discussed in Chapter 4.

4

THEOLOGICAL ARGUMENTS FOR TITHING

INTRODUCTION

This chapter will consider five arguments that are more theological than textual in nature. This means that larger, systematic issues must be considered when evaluating the nature of the argument and its validity.

EXCEEDING RIGHTEOUSNESS ARGUMENT

Christian giving should exceed the giving of the Jews, since Christians have received so much grace. Why would anyone think that the standard has been lowered under grace? There is nowhere in the New Covenant where Jesus is said to have lowered the standard in comparison to the Mosaic Law. Matthew 5:20 says that a Christian's righteousness must exceed the righteousness of the scribes and Pharisees or they will not enter the Kingdom of heaven. How could their righteousness exceed if they are giving less?[39]

---

39 Origen, *Homilies on Numbers* 11.2 (cited by Sharp, "Tithes," 1963); Chrysostom, *The Gospel of Matthew 64.4* (NPNF1 10:395-96); Gordon, *God's Tenth*, 2-4; Robertson, *Five Times Five Points*, 112-13; Leavell, *Training in Stewardship*, 72; Crawford, *Call to Christian Stewardship*, 26; Monroe E. Dodd, *Concerning the Collection: A Manual for Christian Stewardship* (New York: Revell, 1929), 134; Archibald T. Robertson, "Paul's Plans for Raising Money," in *Classic Sermons on Stewardship*, compiled by Warren W. Wiersbe, Kregel Classic Sermons (Grand Rapids: Kregel, 1999) 111; Leewin B. Williams, *Financing the Kingdom* (Grand Rapids: Eerdmans, 1945), 38; J. E. Dillard, ed., *Building a Stewardship Church: A*

To be sure, there are some who reject the requirement of tithing for Christians *and* who appear to lower the standard significantly. However, tithing advocates today appear to be lowering the standard themselves. First, they reject the notion that giving less than under the Mosaic Law could possibly be acceptable to God. But they continue to reference 10 percent of income, even those who recognize the multiple tithes in the Mosaic Law! Once it is recognized that tithing was not 10 percent of income in the Mosaic Law, but closer to 20 percent of crops and cattle produced from the land of Israel, then it becomes difficult to employ this argument.

Rather than talk about whether the standard has been "lowered" or "raised," I prefer the designation of "changed." The standard of giving is different in the New Covenant; it has changed. It's not an issue of "lowered" or "raised," but that Jesus has fulfilled the Law and the Prophets (cf. Matthew 5:17).

Regarding Matthew 5:20, the context of the entire chapter is important for correctly interpreting this verse. First, scribes and Pharisees were known as the most righteous Jews because of their careful observance of the Mosaic Law and their Oral Law. The original audience would have responded in shock to this statement that their "righteousness" was not enough for entrance into the Kingdom. Second, to understand the kind of righteousness intended, careful interpretation of the following antitheses in the remainder of the chapter is necessary. Jesus may be replacing, intensifying, or expounding the Mosaic Law.[40] Third, the main point Jesus is

---

Handbook for Church Workers, 2d ed. (Nashville: Southern Baptist Convention, 1947), 57; Moore, *Found Faithful,* 42; Kauffman, *Challenge of Christian Stewardship,* 88; Hastings, *My Money and God,* 66; Grindstaff, *Principles of Stewardship,* 21; Pink, *Tithing,* 19; Olford, *Grace of Giving,* 42; Gerard Berghoef and Lester DeKoster, *God's Yardstick* (Grand Rapids: Christian's Library, 1980), 71; Alcorn, *Money, Possessions, and Eternity,* 214.

40 David Turner and Darrell L. Bock, *Matthew and Mark,* Cornerstone Biblical Commentary, vol. 11 (Carol Stream, IL: Tyndale House Publishers, 2005), 85.

making is that "Christian discipleship requires a greater righteousness."[41] This demonstrated that everyone was in need of a Savior,
not necessarily that Christians should work harder or try harder.

ARGUMENT FROM THE SABBATH

The law of tithing should be paralleled to the law of the
Sabbath. Just as the Sabbath existed before the Mosaic Law, was
incorporated into the Mosaic Law, and is binding today for Christians, so tithing was before the Mosaic Law, was incorporated into
the Mosaic Law, and is binding for Christians.[42]

Some writers who opposed a tithing mandate have responded
to the Sabbath argument by comparing tithing to circumcision
and blood sacrifices. While both of those are good comparisons
(both were practiced before the Mosaic Law, were incorporated
into the Mosaic Law, and neither are binding for Christians today
in the same way), there is a better comparison: the Levirate Law.
The Levirate Law is defined as follows: when brothers live together
and one of them dies without an heir, one of the surviving brothers
takes his widow to wife, and the first-born of this new marriage is
regarded by law as the son of the deceased. The first-born in this
new marriage is considered, according to law, as the son of the dead
brother. This law is first seen in Genesis 38. It is not described or
explained in any detail, with the apparent assumption that the
original audience would have clearly understood the practice. Onan

---

41 Blomberg, *Matthew*, 105.
42 [Kane], "What We Owe"; Robertson, *Five Times Five Points*, 125;
Charles William Harshman, *Christian Giving* (New York: Eaton and
Mains, 1905), 68; Duncan, *Our Christian Stewardship*, 34, 57; Babbs,
Law of the Tithe, 212; Leavell, *Training in Stewardship*, 19, 68; Dodd,
Concerning the Collection, 185; Lowry, *Should Christians Tithe*, 7; Wil-
liams, *Financing the Kingdom*, 47; Hobbs, *Gospel of Giving*, 14; Kauffman,
Challenge of Christian Stewardship, 60; Tom Rees, *Money Talks* (Frin-
ton-on-Sea, Essex, UK: Hildenborough Hall, [1960-1980]), 33; Pink,
Tithing, 7-8.

understood what was being asked of him. He is commanded to "perform [the] duty" of the levir (Genesis 38:8, HCSB).

Deuteronomy 25:5-10 is the incorporation of this practice into the Mosaic Law. In fact, the law was not peculiar to Israelites, but was practiced by the Assyrians, Hindus (in India), some Brazilians, the Ugarit, Moabites, Elamites, Hittites, New Caledonians, Mongols, Afghans, Abyssinians, and some later American Indians.[43] Its origin is a mystery. When it was added to the Mosaic Law, several modifications were made. It is possible that Ruth 4 contains another example of the Levirate Law.

The Levirate Law is also discussed in the New Testament: Matthew 22:23-28 (paralleled in Mark 12:18-27 and Luke 20:27-38). Jesus is asked a question about the resurrection of the dead by the Sadducees. This provided him the perfect opportunity to abrogate the law. However, since he is living under the Mosaic Law, as are his disciples and the Jews listening to him, he does not address the issue of the binding nature of the law. Verhoef concludes judiciously: "a pre-Mosaic custom does not, as a matter of course, transcend the Old Testament dispensation, becoming an element of the universal and timeless moral code."[44] Thus neither the laws on circumcision nor on the Sabbath are the best parallels for tithing, but instead the Levirate Law. So if the Sabbath laws and tithe laws are still applicable, why not the Levirate Law? This discussion reveals why this type of approach to understanding the Mosaic Laws is problematic.[45]

---

43 See Croteau, *You Mean I Don't Have to Tithe*, 96.

44 Pieter Verhoef, "Tithing: A Hermeneutical Consideration," in *The Law and the Prophets: Old Testament Studies Prepared in Honor of O. T. Allis,* ed. John H. Skilton (Phillipsburg: Presbyterian & Reformed, 1974), 122.

45 For a better approach, see J. Daniel Hays, "Applying the Old Testament Law Today," *Bibliotheca Sacra* 158: 629 (2001): 21-35.

Similarities Between the Levirate Law, the Tithe Laws, Circumcision, and Sabbath

	Levirate law	Tithe laws	Circumcision	Sabbath[46]
Introduced without justification	X	X		
Practiced before the Mosaic Law	X	X	X	X
Obligatory before the Mosaic Law	X		X	X
Widespread; origin unknown	X	X		
Codified, with changes, into the Mosaic Law	X	X		
Practiced outside the Pentateuch (in OT)	X	X	X	X
Received a tract in the Mishnah	X	X		X
NT never explicitly abrogates	X	X		X
Jesus discussed and never abrogated	X	X	X[47]	X

JEROME'S ARGUMENT

The clergy today are in the line of the Levites; their portion is God. Therefore, the clergy today are due tithes just as the Levites were due tithes in the Old Testament.[48] While titled "Jerome's Argument," he is not the only scholar to use this argument. He did

---

46 Some of the conclusions below are controversial. For example, some scholars might say that the New Testament does explicitly abrogate the Sabbath in passages like Romans 14:5-6 or Colossians 2:16-17.

47 See John 7:22-23. Note that while circumcision was incorporated into the Mosaic Law, no significant changes were made (though see Deuteronomy 10:16; 30:6).

48 *The Constitutions of the Holy Apostles* 2.4.25 (ANF 7:408); Jerome, *Letter to Nepotian* (NPNF2 1:91); May, *Law of God on Tithes,* 24; Hensey,

not originate the argument, and he did utilize other arguments. Nonetheless, he is the most prominent proponent of this argument.

The underlying concept to this argument is that the Levitical Tithe is still applicable today, but it is paid to ministers of the gospel (or, the church). However, the three main aspects undergirding the Levitical Tithe have all been fulfilled in the New Covenant: the priesthood, the inheritance, and the temple.

Ministers of the gospel (or, pastors) have not replaced priests. The New Testament envisages the fulfillment of the Mosaic Covenant priesthood in *Christians*, not the pastor. Peter refers to Christians as a "holy priesthood" that was to offer up "spiritual sacrifices" (1 Peter 2:5, HCSB). A few verses later, Peter declares that Christians are a "royal priesthood" and that their purpose is to declare the praises of God (1 Peter 2:9, HCSB). Other passages in the New Testament also describe this fulfillment: Romans 15:16; Hebrews 10:22; and Revelation 5:20; 20:6. Since all Christians have replaced the Levitical priesthood, to claim that pastors are the fulfillment is to compromise the doctrine of the priesthood of believers.

Furthermore, there are two differences between pastors and Levites/priests that should be noted. First, the pastoral role today is typically full-time; priests and Levites served two to three weeks per year in the Temple. Second, priests and Levites were limited in their ability to own property, but pastors today are not limited (nor should they be).

The concept of inheritance is important for understanding the purpose of the tithe in the Mosaic Law. The reason the tribe of Levi was given the tithe is because they were *not* given an inheritance of land (cf. Numbers 18:20-21). Therefore, the tithe should not be considered an earned wage, but as a gift from God. The Israelites needed to keep the Mosaic Law in order to preserve their inheritance (the land) and the Levites needed to fulfill their obligations in order to keep their inheritance (tithes). Besides tithes, the Levites

---

Storehouse Tithing, 49; Hobbs, *Gospel of Giving*, 47; Kauffman, *Challenge of Christian Stewardship*, 65.

also received forty-eight cities, two thousand cubits width of land around each city, and various offerings. Their inheritance was not like their brothers (cf. Deuteronomy 10:9; 14:27; 18:1; Joshua 13:32-33).

In contrast, the New Testament declares that every believer receives the same inheritance in the New Covenant: Acts 20:32; 26:18; Galatians 3:18; Ephesians 1:11-12, 14; 5:5; Colossians 1:12; 3:24; Hebrews 9:15; 1 Peter 1:4. All of these passages refer to inheritance as a future salvation. Acts 20:32 is particularly important because Paul is addressing the elders of the church in Ephesus. He told them that they would receive an "inheritance among all who are sanctified" (HCSB). Rather than a distinct inheritance like the Levites, pastors receive the same inheritance as all Christians. The important concept of inheritance, which undergirded the Levitical Tithe, has been fulfilled in the New Covenant.

Finally, the Levitical Tithe was used for the support of the temple in Jerusalem (cf. Nehemiah 10). Some tithing advocates claim that the temple in the Old Testament has been replaced by the Church in the New Testament. Is this what Scripture explains?

While the temple as a *building* does not continue into the New Covenant, the *concept* of the temple does continue. There are two aspects to the fulfillment of the temple in the New Testament: through Christ and through Christians. In John 2:19-21, John interprets Jesus' words about the temple so that Jesus was actually referencing his body. In John 4:21-24, Jesus' answer to the Samaritan woman's question about the place of worship makes it clear that Jesus himself would become the new center of worship. Christians, both corporately and individually, also fulfill the concept of temple in the New Testament. Paul refers to the corporate body of believers in 1 Corinthians 3:16-17 as "a temple of God" (NASB). In 1 Corinthians 6:19, Paul appears to be referring to each individual believer as "a temple of the Holy Spirit who is in you" (NASB). While the temple in the Old Testament was the place where God dwelled, now his Spirit dwells within each believer.

Therefore, all of the concepts underlying the Levitical Tithe have been fulfilled in the New Covenant. Pastors are not the continuation of the line of neither the Levites nor priests. To argue that pastors should receive tithes like the Levites is neither a compelling nor plausible argument.

MORAL LAW ARGUMENT

The Mosaic Law should be understood as having three parts: moral, civil, and ceremonial. Tithing is part of the moral law and therefore continues.[49] One way this argument is used is that the tithe "Terumah" specifies that the Levitical Tithe in Leviticus 27 and Numbers 18 is part of the moral law.[50]

Many Christians are familiar with the Mosaic Law being broken into three parts: the tri-partite view. Most proponents of the tri-partite view of the Mosaic Law believe that the civil law only applied to Israel and the ceremonial law was fulfilled in Christ. Therefore, only the moral law continues.

Even if I accept the three-fold division (which I do not), this argument has significant issues.[51] Primarily, which tithe law is specifically part of the moral law and why? The Levitical Tithe is connected to a host of ceremonial aspects of the Mosaic Law

---

49 Hensey, *Storehouse Tithing,* 49; P. E. Burroughs, *The Grace of Giving* (Nashville: Sunday School Board of the Southern Baptist Convention, 1934), 58; Lowry, *Should Christians Tithe,* 7; Dillard, *Building a Stewardship Church,* 61; Muncy, *Fellowship with God,* 131; Rice, *All about Christian Giving,* 23; Clearwaters, *Stewardship Sermonettes,* 115; Howard Foshee, "The Tithe," in *Encyclopedia of Southern Baptists,* ed. Norman Wade Cox, 2 vols. (Nashville: Broadman, 1958), 1418; Ben Gill, *Stewardship: The Biblical Basis for Living* (Arlington: Summit, 1996), 62; Holmes, "Tithing," 48.

50 See N. L. Rigby, *Christ Our Creditor: "How Much Owest Thou?" or The Tithe Terumoth: Its Philosophy, History and Perpetuity* (Murray, KY: News and Truth Publishing, [1895-1899]), 41.

51 See William D. Barrick, "The Mosaic Covenant," *Master's Seminary Journal* 10, no. 2 (Fall 1999): 230-32, for more discussion on this.

(utilizing the terminology of tri-partite proponents), including the temple, the Levites, and the priests. The Festival Tithe is also connected to ceremonial aspects of the Mosaic Law, including the feasts of Passover, Tabernacles, and Pentecost. The Charity Tithe is probably part of the civil law, but even if it were part of the moral law, this tithe is only required once every three years.

Some tithing advocates have argued that the reference to the tithe as a "terumah" in Numbers 18:24-29 is what places the Levitical Tithe into the category of moral law. They say that this Hebrew word *terumah* is what distinguishes the Levitical Tithe from all other tithes.[52] This concept of *terumah* is sadly misguided and using the Hebrew word this way is uninformed. *Terumah* means a contribution or offering for sacred purposes.[53] It is used first in Exodus 25:2-3 (three times) in reference to the offering taken for the Tabernacle. It is also used in Exodus 29, 30, 35, and 36 where it has no relationship to tithes. It also occurs in Leviticus 7, 10, 22 with no reference to tithes. Rigby presented this word as if its use in Numbers 18 separates it as a technical term relating it to the moral law. However, *terumah* is used to refer to ceremonial aspects of the law, such as in Leviticus 7:14: "From the cakes he must present one portion of each offering as a contribution to the LORD. It will belong to the priest who sprinkles the blood of the fellowship offering; it is his" (HCSB). The word translated "contribution" is the Hebrew word *terumah*. Leviticus 7:14 appears to reference an aspect of the law that is clearly not moral (in the tripartite system). Therefore, this use of the "Tithe Terumah" is ultimately unpersuasive.

---

52 Ibid.

53 See Francis Brown, S. R. Driver, and Charles A. Briggs, *A Hebrew and English Lexicon of the Old Testament*, trans. by Edward Robinson (Oxford: Clarendon Press, 1906), 929.

NATURAL LAW ARGUMENT
(OR, THE ARGUMENT FROM ORIGIN)

Since tithing was practiced before the Mosaic Law and by almost all nations in the history of the world, it is a part of natural law or is a universal law. The only explanation for the origin of tithing is either as a direct command from God at the beginning or that all people have the innate sense planted within them by God that they should give 10 percent.[54]

This is primarily an appeal to the question of the origin of tithing: where did it come from? While it was surely practiced by most nations in the history of the world, is an appeal to natural law (or a direct command from God) the only other explanation?

First, if the Mosaic Law was "pre-revealed," that is, if it was disclosed prior to the time of Moses and could be dated back to Adam and his sons, but Scripture left out that event, then I would expect the actions of the characters in the Genesis narratives between the Fall and Sinai to reflect this. Some texts argue against a pre-Sinai revealing of the Law. First, the Mosaic Law commands murderers to be punished by death; God forbade that in Cain's case. Second, Abraham did not give the prescribed amount according to the Mosaic Law when winning spoils in war (cf. Numbers 31). Third,

---

54 Speer, *God's Rule for Christian Giving,* 102; [Kane], "What We Owe"; Watson, *Soul Food,* 99; Robertson, *Five Times Five Points,* 116; Rigby, *Christ Our Creditor,* 17; Shaw, *God's Financial Plan,* 46-47; Stewart, *Tithe,* 40-42; Lansdell, *Sacred Tenth,* 1-38, 48-51, 54; Duncan, *Our Christian Stewardship,* 47-48; Babbs, *Law of the Tithe,* 24; Lovejoy, *Stewardship for All of Life,* 90-91; Lowry, *Should Christians Tithe,* 6; Salstrand, *Tithe,* 15-18; Dillard, *Good Stewards,* 82; Harrell, *Stewardship and the Tithe,* 40; Hobbs, *Gospel of Giving,* 14; Clearwaters, *Stewardship Sermonettes,* 25; Kauffman, *Challenge of Christian Stewardship,* 61; Rees, *Money Talks,* 31; Pink, *Tithing,* 18; Wester, "Christian and the Tithe," 160; Kendall, *Tithing,* 52-55; Watley, *Bring the Full Tithe,* 14; Gill, *Stewardship,* 60; David M. James, "Christian Giving," *Living Orthodoxy* 21, no. 4 (2000): 8.

Genesis 9:3 gives permission for every animal to be eaten; the Mosaic Law explicitly forbade that (cf. Leviticus 11:1-44). These are merely three examples that demonstrate that a manifestation of the Mosaic Law at (or near) the Fall is problematic.

The following four brief points on the Mosaic Law and natural law in the New Testament will be helpful to consider. First, Romans 1:20-21 and 2:14-15 appear to be describing something that is similar to natural law and/or general revelation. Second, Romans 5:12-14 declares that there was a time before law was given. Third, Galatians 3:17 says that 430 years after Abraham the Law came. Fourth, Galatians 3:19 says that the law was added; for it to have been added, it could not have previously been revealed.

The basic argument that tithing is a part of natural law is that so many nations and societies have practiced it. However, the evidence proves *too much*. While it is true that a *form* of tithing was practiced by many nations and societies, the specifics of that practice are typically (but not always) ignored. For example, in Arabia tithes were paid on frankincense, but on ground that was watered by rain (that is, by their god Baal) 20 percent was due: a double tithe.[55] Each nation and society had radically different rules and laws related to "tithing." Some items were subject to tithes, others were not. Sometimes items had to be "double tithed" (that is, 20 percent), sometimes not. In fact, the differences far outweigh the similarities.[56] This information significantly weakens the natural law argument.

So if the Mosaic Law (and, therefore, tithing) was not revealed pre-Sinai, then what, besides "natural law," could explain the proliferation of tithing among societies? One tithing advocate declared that 10 percent did not come from the fingers on our hands; the Sabbath, he said, was not every seventh day because the knuckles

---

55 Lansdell, *Sacred Tenth*, 17.

56 See Croteau, *You Mean I Don't Have to Tithe*, 89-90. For information on the Gentile practice of tithing (Egyptian, Babylonian, Persian, Phoenician, Arabian, Greek, Roman, Pelasgi, Sicilians and more) see Landsell, *Sacred Tenth*, 1-38.

of a man's hand have seven elevations and depressions.[57] Several scholars, however, find the "ten finger" argument compelling. Mac-Culloch thinks tithing is "probably" related to early views about numbers and is connected to fingers and toes.[58] Rouse said there is "no doubt" that it is connected to a tenth being an easy fraction to calculate.[59] Finally, Morley says that tithing was common "apparently" because people counted using the base of ten, "based on ten fingers."[60] While some might object that having ten fingers is a trite explanation for the preponderance of tithing practices, it remains a better option than the thesis that tithing was part of natural law or that God revealed the tithe law from the beginning.

CONCLUSION

Five theological arguments have been considered. The standard of giving has not been lowered or raised in the New Covenant; it has changed. Matthew 5:20 is not a compelling argument for giving at least 10 percent, since the Jews gave at least 20 percent. The Sabbath is not a very good parallel for tithing; the Levirate Law is a better parallel and favors the discontinuation of the practice. Ministers of the gospel (or, the clergy) are not the replacement for the Levites or priests. Even if the Mosaic Law should be viewed as having three parts, connecting any of the tithe laws to the moral law is a stretch. Finally, it cannot be demonstrated that tithing was given as a command at the Fall or that it is a part of natural law. If there is not one specific text in the Old or New Testament that demonstrates that Christians are required to give 10 percent of income, and if there is not a persuasive theological argument, could there be a compelling argument from Church history?

---

57 See Speer, *God's Rule for Christian Giving,* 253.

58 J. A. MacCulloch, "Tithes," in *Encyclopædia of Religion and Ethics,* ed. James Hastings (New York: Scribner, 1951), 347.

59 W. H. D. Rouse, "Tithes (Greek)," in *Encyclopædia of Religion and Ethics,* ed. James Hastings (New York: Scribner, 1951), 350.

60 Brian K. Morley, "Tithe, Tithing," in *Evangelical Dictionary of Biblical Theology,* ed. Walter A. Elwell (Grand Rapids: Baker, 1996), 779.

5

Historical Arguments for Tithing

Introduction

Historical theology deserves a seat at the table of theological debate. While the current topic does not provide the opportunity for discussing how historical theology can be overly minimized or depended upon too strongly, a discussion on tithing without considering the historical theological question would leave the current study anemic. Two closely related arguments need to be considered in this brief chapter: the Continuity Argument and the Historical Argument.

The Continuity Argument

The people of God have always given a tenth and Christians should give a tenth also.[61] Why would someone want to change now, after thousands of years, what God's people have always done and should continue to do?

While I was on a radio show a caller explained how frustrated he was with scholars who seem to come up with new views just so they can publish books. The show's host then asked me to respond. The assumption in that question is that the view that I propose is "new." While there might be aspects of my argument that are unique, the basic thrust of what I am proposing here (and in my other publications on this topic) is not new at all!

---

61 Duncan, *Our Christian Stewardship*, 15-16; Charles Stanley, *The Glorious Journey* (Nashville: Nelson, 1996), 505.

Have the "people of God" always given a tenth? First, the phrase the "people of God" appears to be a reference to those who throughout history have been followers of the God of the Bible, whether it is those before the Mosaic Law, like Noah and Abraham, those during the Mosaic Law, like Joshua and David, or those in the New Covenant, Christians from Paul to Billy Graham.

Second, there is no evidence that followers of God gave 10 percent of their income on any kind of consistent basis during any period of church history. Before the Mosaic Law there are two references to tithing: Abraham (Genesis 14:18-20) and Jacob (Genesis 28:22). The passage about Abraham explains that he gave 100 percent of the spoils of war, but it says nothing about him giving 10 percent to Melchizedek or any other priest at any other time. Jacob promises to give a tenth if God fulfills His promise to Jacob, but: first, Genesis never describes Jacob actually giving this tithe; second, Genesis never explains to whom he could give it; and third, Jacob would not have given the tithe for over twenty years, since that is how long it took before God's promises came to pass.

In the Mosaic Law, the Israelites did not give 10 percent of income, but averaged at least 20 percent per year from crops and cattle. This is based on the multiple tithes that they would give each year. There is no direct, explicit evidence that Christians in the New Testament were giving 10 percent of their income to the church. This is not to say that they were not, but the evidence for either view is lacking.

When examining church history, it is clear that not all of God's people have had the same mindset on tithing. But more on this will be said in addressing the Historical Argument below. Both of these arguments bleed over into each other, though they are not saying the exact same thing.

THE HISTORICAL ARGUMENT

Tithing is a well-tested, ancient form of giving that has been validated throughout Church history.[62] Most of the great leaders in church history, if not all of them, advocated tithing for Christians. The practice has been successfully taught and practiced for two thousand years throughout church history.

It is true that most, even the majority, of church leaders have advocated tithing. However, while some scholars have tried to paint the picture as if tithing were the *only* view held to throughout church history, this is clearly not the case. There were church leaders on both sides of this issue. While this is not the place for a detailed treatment, a few highlights over the past two thousand years should prove useful.[63]

The controversy did not escape the third century, as Clement of Alexandria (d. 215) was an advocate for Christians being required to give 10 percent of their income, while Origen (d. 255) was against the idea. A document called the *Didascalia Apostolorum* was against the binding nature of tithing. In the fourth century, Epiphanius (370) was against the requirement of tithing, while several others were for it, including Hilary of Poitiers (366), Basil of Caesarea (370), Ambrose (374), and a document called the *Apostolic Constitutions*.

There are three other individuals from this same period that should be mentioned, as they are important men in church history and their specific views on tithing have been, sometimes, too quickly referenced: John Chrysostom (375), Jerome (385), and Augustine (400). While all of these men advocated tithing, the way they arrived at this conclusion is very different from most

---

62 Lansdell, *Sacred Tenth,* 180-240; Babbs, *Law of the Tithe,* 143-50; Salstrand, *Tithe,* 39-43; Dillard, *Good Stewards,* 80; Hobbs, *Gospel of Giving,* 14; Clearwaters, *Stewardship,* 26; Kauffman, *Challenge of Christian Stewardship,* 72-74; Alcorn, *Money, Possessions, and Eternity,* 216.

63 For references for all of the following, see Croteau, *You Mean I Don't Have to Tithe,* Appendix A-B. For more details, see Chapter 2 in the same book.

tithing advocates today. All three of them believed that the standard for Christian giving was much more than 10 percent of income; however, since Christians were not even giving what the Jews were required to give (10 percent), they were willing to compromise the real teaching of the New Testament[64] and settle for 10 percent of income. By doing this, Christians would then at least be giving as much as the Israelites did under the Mosaic Law.[65]

For the next several centuries the evidence shows a prevailing advocacy for tithing, with no significant opponents appearing on the scene. Some of the more prominent names from this time period include Cassian (410), Severinus (550), Pope Gregory the Great (600), and Charlemagne (770).

Between 1000 and the Reformation, many leaders took opposing views on this issue. The Waldenses (ca. 12th century), Thomas Aquinas (d. 1275), John Wycliff (d. 1384), John Huss (d. 1415), and Erasmus (d. 1536) all believed that Christians were not required to tithe. However, Edward (1050), William the Conqueror (1066) and Bernard of Clairvaux (1139) disagreed.

Around the time of the Reformation, several scholars weighed in on this issue. Martin Luther (d. 1546), the Anabaptists (ca. 1525), John Smyth (1609), who is typically credited with being the first Baptist, Roger Williams (ca. 1636), who is typically credited with being the first Baptist in America, John Owen (1680), and John Bunyan (d. 1688) all argued that tithing was connected to the Mosaic Law and Christians were not required to tithe. However, both Matthew Henry (d. 1714) and Increase Mather (d. 1723) disagreed.

From this point on, many church leaders have been on both sides of the issue. With men like John Gill, (d. 1771), Charles Spurgeon (d. 1892), G. Campbell Morgan (1898), R. C. H. Lenski (1946), Lewis Sperry Chafer (1948), Ray Stedman (1951),

---

64 They believed that the New Testament taught that all Christians were to sell everything they had and give the money to the poor.

65 As stated above (cf. the Exceeding Righteousness Argument), this reasoning is problematic.

Charles Ryrie (1969), Garry Friesen (1980), John MacArthur (1982), Paul Fink (1982), Charles Swindoll (1990), and J. Vernon McGee (1991) arguing against the direct applicability of tithing for Christians, and Cotton Mather (1833), Charles Finney (d. 1875), Thomas Kane (1876), Henry Lansdell (1906), Billy Graham (1953), Herschel Hobbs (1954), John R. Rice (1954), A. W. Pink (1967), Elmer Towns (1975), W. A. Criswell (1980), John Piper (1981), R. T. Kendall (1982), Randy Alcorn (1989), Larry Burkett (1991), Charles Stanley (1996), David Jeremiah (2002), Ken Hemphill (2006), and Howard Dayton (2009) all believing that Christians are mandated to tithe.

So, what should be taken from this (very) brief historical survey? First, Christians, even great scholars, have disagreed over this issue throughout the past 2000 years, so dividing fellowship over the issue of tithing is unnecessary. Second, the question cannot be settled in historical theology. Scripture is the final authority for all Christians, and therefore the matter needs to be settled by the teaching of God's Word. Third, while many have supported tithing, the list against tithing is impressive and should not be ignored. At the very least, this list should cause everyone to rethink the issue and really try to understand what God's Word says about this issue.

CONCLUSION

Neither of the arguments based on church history stand up to scrutiny. The views about tithing have been diverse. Therefore, there is no consistent pattern of thinking on this issue throughout the past 2000 years. Any argument based on the concept that tithing is required because of tradition or church history needs to look again at the data and various views that have been advocated.

6

EXPERIENTIAL ARGUMENTS FOR TITHING

INTRODUCTION

While biblical, theological, and historical arguments are the kinds of arguments that are convincing to some people, others find the experiential or pragmatic arguments more convincing. For some, while it is important to know and understand what Scripture teaches on a subject, how it works out in "real life" is just as important, if not more so. Three arguments fit in this category of experiential arguments for the continuation of tithing.

THE ANECDOTAL ARGUMENT

God has significantly blessed those who have faithfully tithed. This blessing demonstrates that tithing is his method for giving in the current period.[66]

In fact, some ministries have offered to give "refunds" if after a certain period (like ninety days) they are not in a better financial situation after giving tithing a try. Other preachers have stated that no one ever has financial trouble if they are tithing. I've even heard one preacher say that no one has *ever* gone bankrupt while tithing!

Has anyone who faithfully tithed gone bankrupt? Absolutely! There are many news stories on the internet explaining how certain individuals have gone bankrupt while tithing. While the situation of Evander Holyfield might seem like the exception, the reality is that so many have had this issue of going bankrupt while tithing

---

66 Ralph S. Cushman and Martha F. Bellinger, *Adventures in Stewardship* (New York: Abingdon, 1919), 11; see also the anonymous *I Tithe Joyfully! A Book of Letters from Those Who Do* (Chicago: Moody, 1960).

that the federal government has been wrestling with how to adjudicate this situation. President Clinton signed the Religious Liberty and Charitable Donation Protection Act in 1998 to allow those who are bankrupt to continue tithing. But a 2005 law overturned that decision: the Bankruptcy Abuse Prevention and Consumer Protection Act. The fact that the federal government has had to monitor this so much demonstrates that this is not a rare situation. To give my own "anecdotal argument," I've had a friend who was giving about 18 percent of his income, and his financial situation continued to deteriorate more and more. Finally, in order to go to seminary, he filed for bankruptcy. He declared how good God was in taking care of him, but really the federal government bailed him out.

Why is it that so many people are "blessed" when they tithe? While the question may be impossible to answer in every case, it seems that when people learn to live off 90 percent of their income (or less), when they are meticulous with where their money is going, they are better stewards over the resources God gives them. In other words, if they meticulously gave 10 percent, they would be better stewards than those who were not careful with their finances. The reason for the blessing is their obedience to biblical principles of stewardship and giving, not following the modern teaching on giving 10 percent of income.

THE CONCESSION ARGUMENT

Christians are required to give all: "Sell all that you have and distribute it to the poor" (Luke 18:22, HCSB). However, Christians have failed to live in obedience to Jesus' command. Therefore, they should at least give 10 percent, the standard under the Mosaic Law.

As mentioned already, three ancient advocates for tithing have used this argument: John Chrysostom, Jerome, and Augustine. It's important to note not only *that* these three advocated tithing, but the way they arrived at their conclusion.[67] Jerome said that Jesus' command quoted above was for all Christians. However, since Christians were unwilling to do that, they should "imitate the rudimentary teaching of the Jews" by giving 10 percent of their income to the poor and the clergy.[68] Augustine noticed that Christians were not currently paying their tithes. He utilized the text from Luke 18:22 and declared that as binding for all Christians. But, since they were unwilling to obey Jesus' command in Luke 18, they should be commanded to imitate the Jews and *at least* give 10 percent of their income.[69]

The argument for the tithe here fascinates me, especially because so many tithing advocates cite Jerome and Augustine for support (probably without knowing *how* they arrived at their conclusion). In response to this line of thinking, several thoughts should be considered. First, Jews did not give 10 percent of income. If Christians need to give "at least" what the Jews gave, then the standard is not 10 percent, but closer to 20 percent. Second, if the requirement is to sell everything and give it to the poor, then lowering that standard is totally unacceptable. Why is it okay to lower the requirements of a biblical command because Christians refuse to obey it? Third, is Luke 18:22 a requirement for all Christians? Stein responds to this thought by stating that the command was not required for salvation, but that it illustrated the type of commitment that was necessary if one was to follow Jesus.[70] Furthermore, not only does this mode of interpretation fall for the "description

67 This connects the Concession Argument with some of the historical arguments from the previous chapter.

68 Sharp, "Tithes," 1964. Jerome also commends Christians to tithe in his *Commentary on Matthew 2.22* (cited by Stuart Murray, Beyond Tithing [Carlisle, UK: Paternoster, 2000], 117).

69 Augustine, *On the Psalms: Psalm 147* 13 *(NPNF1* 8:668). In Augustine's writings, he discussed the scribes and Pharisees, for the most part, as if they gave only 10 percent. See comments in Augustine, *Sermon 35 (NPNF1* 6:367-68); *Sermon 56 (NPNF1* 6:435-36). See also comments in Justo Gonzalez, *Faith and Wealth* (San Francisco: Harper, 1990), 219.

70 See Stein, *Luke*, 456.

equals prescription" fallacy, but it ignores the context of Luke 19 (especially verses 8-9), where Zacchaeus gave away half of his possessions and Jesus declared that salvation had come to his house.

The Pragmatic Argument

Tithing is a very easy to understand method of giving. It is also easy to calculate, by taking your paycheck and multiplying it by 0.1. It is also very systematic, which is helpful for church's budgets. It is really the only reasonable method of giving based upon Scripture.[71]

Ultimately, this issue should not depend upon what is easy to understand or to obey, but by what the Bible teaches. I admit that putting your paycheck into a calculator and multiplying that by 0.1 is easy. However, I believe that Scripture presents God as pursuing a relationship with people, not as God hoping his people have a relationship with a calculator.

This argument seems to indicate that there really is no other option, no other way or method that could be culled from the pages of Scripture. Without the mandate to tithe, will Christians be left wondering how much to give, having no clue to an amount? Is this valid? The following chapter will explain that there are many principles to guide giving for Christians. The principles will not be as easy as giving 10 percent of income, but they are scriptural principles that, when applied, will draw people into a closer relationship with their God. Easy is not always better, and it definitely is not always biblical. So, what would a biblical model of giving look like? Chapter 7 answers that question.

---

71 Williams, *Financing the Kingdom*, 42; Dillard, *Good Stewards*, 90-91; Powell, *Money and the Church*, 224-25.

7

Giving After The Cross

Introduction

Is there any standard for giving today? Are Christians left to their feelings, emotions, impulses, or mystical experiences? Far from it! God has graciously provided many principles for giving in Scripture. The most important category for giving is the foundational element found in the Bible that has to do with the correct mindset a Christian should have. A second category involves evaluating the motivations for giving. If the motivation is wrong, then the entire process may be skewed. The foundational principles are those that seem to "push" us in giving, while the motivation principles seem to "pull" us. Third, certain details regarding giving are important to consider before the amount itself is decided upon. Fourth, the attitude a Christian has toward giving (and their possessions) will significantly impact their manner in giving. The category most people are interested in, which will be discussed fifth, is the amount of giving: how much should a Christian give? Is it a certain amount or a certain percentage? I'll forewarn you: don't expect a formulaic answer.

Christian giving is an act of worship. Worshiping God and bringing glory to him in all that we do should penetrate every area of our lives. Some people have expressed to me that when they got baptized, they left their wallet at home. Christians should not have segmented, disconnected areas in their lives, where they hold back certain areas from Christ's lordship. He is Lord over all of our lives, and all of our lives should be lived out in worship to him.

THE DRIVING FORCE OF GIVING

What should be driving the giving of a Christian's financial resources to a ministry? I was at a church once that sent out an email the last week of December to remind the church members that December 31st was the last day to give and still receive a tax break for that tax year. The contributions that came in during that week made it the highest offering the church took all year! While there is nothing wrong with getting a tax deduction for charitable giving, is that a biblical foundation for giving? Not in the Bible! There are three principles that should drive every aspect of giving, three principles that should inform every category that will be discussed in this chapter, and all three are found in 2 Corinthians 8-9. These are the foundations for giving.

First, Christian giving should be *grace-driven*: giving is a response to the grace of God shown to believers. Grace and giving are the overarching themes tied together in 2 Corinthians 8-9. Paul uses the Greek word for grace (*charis*) eighteen times in 2 Corinthians, and ten of the eighteen are in these two chapters. In 8:1, Paul begins by framing the entire discussion about the sacrificial and generous giving among the Macedonians by referring to it as "the grace of God." He refers to their contributions to help the poor saints in Jerusalem as an "act of grace" three times (2 Corinthians 8:6, 7, 19). But how does *grace* become a driving force in Christian giving?

We need to take more time to meditate on God's grace. The more we recognize that we have done nothing to deserve salvation, nothing to work our way into a right relationship with God, that we were utterly dead in trespasses and sins before God initiated a relationship with us, the more thankful and grateful we should become. God did not pour out a small drop of grace on us. Notice that 2 Corinthians 9:14 refers to the "surpassing grace of God." The Greek word for surpassing refers to "a degree that extraordinarily exceeds a point on a scale of extent."[72] Paul uses a similar phrase in Ephesians 2:7 when he refers to the "surpassing riches of his grace." The same Greek word is used for "surpassing," but he adds "riches," referring to the abundant nature of God's grace. When we begin to come to grip with God's grace, it should create such a well of thankfulness that we desire to worship God through giving. Grace should be a driving force of giving.

Second, Christian giving should be *relationship-driven*: giving is based upon one's relationship with the Lord. In 2 Corinthians 8:5, Paul describes the Macedonians as first giving themselves "to the Lord." This is not simply a reference to temporal sequence, but mainly to priority or prominence. We should place our relationship with Christ above all other aspects of our lives. When we spend time with the Lord, seeking the Lord for wisdom, praising the Lord for all the blessings he has poured out upon us, adoring the Lord for who he is, we *will* be changed. While our desires were consumed with selfish thoughts and arrogant ponderings, God has poured out his grace upon us in order for us to walk in the good works that God has prepared for us to do (cf. Ephesians 2:10). That is why Paul can say that generous giving proves the genuineness of a Christian's love for God (2 Corinthians 8:8). An intimate relationship with the Lord will drive generous Christian giving.

Third, Christian giving should be *love-driven:* giving is a demonstration of a Christian's love. Paul builds off the concept of love in 2 Corinthians 8:8 and continues in verse 9 by providing an example of giving that is driven by love: Jesus gave of himself. Paul's reference to love in 8:8 is what prompted this example. Giving everything one has without love results in nothing (cf. 1 Corinthians 13:3). Jesus' death on the cross was the ultimate demonstration of love (cf. 1 John 4:9-10). As we meditate upon the grace of God and as we pursue God with all our heart, soul, mind, and strength, God will fill us with his love so that we can then pour this love out

---

72 Walter Bauer, *A Greek-English Lexicon of the New Testament and other Early Christian Literature*, 3d ed, rev. and ed. F. W. Danker, W. F. Arndt, and F. W. Gingrich (Chicago: University of Chicago Press, 2000), 1032.

on those around us. One of the manifestations of Christian love is generous giving, which is why the New Testament has a great concern for the sin of greed.[73] Lutheran clergyman and theologian John Mueller concludes: "It is only at the foot of the blood-stained cross of Calvary that the believer learns the art of Christian giving."[74] Christian giving should be driven by love.

THE MOTIVATIONS FOR GIVING

The motivations that underlie Christian giving are important to consider. Jesus himself addressed the issue in Matthew 6:1-4. In that section of the Sermon on the Mount, Jesus is teaching his disciples and the crowds that they should not be motivated to give to the needy in order to be seen by others. The principle underlying the passage is *not* that if others find out you have given (by you telling them or by other means), that you will have no reward, but that if the motivation of your heart is to be seen by them, then you will have no reward. So, what are some positive motivations for giving? There are four principles that motivate Christian giving.

First, thankfulness to God the Father and the Lord Jesus Christ should motivate giving: as a Christian grows in their thankfulness to God, his or her giving should grow as well. It is hard to imagine that we have a truly thankful heart for all we have, for all God has given us, but then we remain stingy in our giving. As Paul is compelling the church in Corinth to fulfill their words with a generous contribution to help the poor saints in Jerusalem, he describes the giving in terms of "many acts of thanksgiving to God" (2 Corinthians 9:12, HCSB). Paul commanded that we be thankful (Colossians 3:15; 1 Thessalonians 5:18). And in Philippians 4:18 Paul lives out these words as he shows himself thankful to the church at Philippi for their generous gift to him.

73 See Matthew 23:25; Luke 11:39; 1 Corinthians 5:10, 11; 6:10; Ephesians 4:19; 1 Timothy 3:8; Titus 1:7; 2 Peter 2:3.
74 John Theodore Mueller, *Christian Dogmatics: A Handbook of Doctrinal Theology for Pastors, Teachers, and Laymen* (St. Louis: Concordia, 1934), 415.

Second, since Christians should desire to grow spiritually, knowing that giving causes growth in good works should motivate more abundant giving. According to Ephesians 2, God poured his grace upon us in order for him to receive glory and praise (2:7) and for the purpose that we will walk in the good works that God prepared for us to do. As we are obedient to the New Testament principles of giving, we will grow in good works. In 2 Corinthians 9:8, Paul mentions the concept of sowing and reaping: if a farmer believes that it is a waste to sow seed, then that farmer will have very little to reap. Applied to giving, the more generous and sacrificial we are in our giving, the more plentiful harvest we will reap. Does this refer to a spiritual or material harvest? Is it now or later? Second Corinthians 9:6 references "every good deed" (NASB) and 9:9 mentions "righteousness." These clues seem to suggest that as we give generously, God will increase our righteousness and we will be better equipped to serve him faithfully. Therefore, Christians will reap a spiritual harvest now as we obey the principles in the New Testament about giving. Thus we will be "conformed to the image of His Son" (Romans 8:29, HCSB), which should be the desire of every Christian's heart.

Third, a Christian should be motivated by the praise of his God. Hearing the words "Well done, good and faithful slave" (Matthew 25:21, HCSB) should be a motivator for all of the Christian life. It is appropriate to dwell upon the idea that God praises sacrificial giving. In Mark 12:42-44, the widow gave "two lepta," which is equal to less than ten minutes worth of an average workers daily pay. The amount she put in is significant because Jesus says she put in *all* she had. Therefore, this poor widow did not have much, but gave sacrificially, and this sacrificial giving is praised by Jesus. Another example of sacrificial giving is seen in 2 Corinthians 8:2-3. Paul praises the Macedonian churches for giving "beyond their ability." He praises neither the proportion nor the amount of their gift, but the sacrificial nature and heart (or, eagerness) with which they gave. For this, Paul praises them. Just like a child loves to hear the praise of her loving parent, so should we be motivated to give in order to hear the praise of our heavenly Father.

Fourth, a Christian should be motivated by future rewards: Christian giving stores up eternal rewards for the one giving. We need to stay cognizant that even though a sacrifice might be made in this life regarding desires or comforts, an eternal investment is made. Matthew 6:19-21 appears[75] to contain a motivation by discussing the concept of storing up treasures in heaven. It is, therefore, not inappropriate to consider giving as a way to receive rewards in the future; Jesus himself gives this as a motivation.

THE DETAILS OF GIVING

Some specific principles can be gleaned from the New Testament that will inform us about several aspects of giving. These details answer many of the questions I get asked in Q&A sessions. These three principles should be remembered when considering who should give, when someone should give, and how the collection should be taken.

Supporting the local church is the obligation of every believer.[76] The requirement to give is not isolated to the rich only, but extends to all Christians. In 1 Corinthians 16:2, each believer is exhorted to be involved with the collection for the poor saints in Jerusalem. The church at Corinth probably included women and slaves, and they are included in this exhortation. Paul does not command a certain amount to be given, but does encourage everyone

---

75 There are differing views on the interpretation of these verses. For two opposing views, see Randy Alcorn, *Law of Rewards: Giving What You Can't Keep to Gain What You Can't Lose* (Wheaton: Tyndale, 2003); Craig L. Blomberg, "Degrees of Reward in the Kingdom of Heaven," *JETS* 35 (1992): 159-72.

76 James Edward Anderson, "Priorities in Christian Giving" (Th.M. thesis, Dallas Theological Seminary, 1967), 4, concludes the following order in the priorities for giving: "(1) destitute relatives, (2) spiritual ministries, and (3) needy individuals." His discussion has been beneficial in the formation of some of my thoughts on prioritizing giving.

to be involved, no matter the amount of the gift. Remember the widow's gift in Mark 12:42-44: the sacrificial nature and heart of the giver is important, not the amount of the gift. The exhortation to give is *universal*, even if the amount is very minimal.

In the same verse, Paul encourages systematic giving: "on the first day of every week." By setting aside a contribution on a regular basis, be it weekly, bi-monthly, or monthly, the Christian is giving in accordance with Paul's exhortation. Does it have to be *every* week? First, it should be remembered that churches have bills regularly, so we should at least consider the church's bills in deciding on how often we will give. Second, the underlying principle is the concept of systematic, regular giving. It is probably a wise idea for several reasons. For example, the concept of giving cheerfully (which will be discussed below) could easily get compromised if the giver finds himself putting such a large amount that covers months' worth of giving. Also, it is amazing at how quickly giving can add up when done regularly. Giving a modest amount weekly or monthly becomes a significant amount at the end of the year. Therefore, every Christian should be involved in contributing to their local church on a regular, systematic basis.

Finally, certain precautions should be used with the handling of money. Some Christians have communicated to me their hesitancy about giving to their local church because of the misuse of funds. Notice that in 2 Corinthians 8:16-21, Paul points out that Titus and another brother, who is famous for his work "in the gospel," is being sent to collect the contributions. Money can be a sensitive issue, so proper precautions were taken to assure that whatever was collected was being used for the intended purpose. Transparency by those who are asking for contributions is a very important concept.

THE ATTITUDE OF GIVING AND POSSESSIONS

Four principles need to accompany our worship through giving. As these four concepts are joined to giving, they create a powerful impact on the life of the Christian, as they assure that the giving is done with the right attitude.

Giving should never have to be compelled, but should be done out of our free volition. The concept of voluntary contributions is rich in the history of stewardship research, but it can easily be neglected when finances are tight in a church. Regardless, Paul clearly describes the Macedonian giving in this way: of their own accord or voluntarily (2 Corinthians 8:3). This rare word also occurs later in the same chapter in describing Titus' eagerness to take part in the collection. While Paul's description is compelling, his directive in 2 Corinthians 9:7 is more direct: giving is not to be done from pressure or compulsion, but voluntarily. This leads into the next concept.

Rather than having to be compelled to give, giving should be intentional: a Christian should seek opportunities and give deliberately in order to meet a genuine need, not out of guilt or merely to soothe a pressing request. Returning to 2 Corinthians 8, Paul describes the Macedonians in verse 4 as begging them for the opportunity to be involved in the contributions being collected for the saints in Jerusalem. The Macedonians are praised for being eager and intentional in their giving (cf. Romans 15:26-28). In 2 Corinthians 9:2, Paul now praises the Corinthians for their eagerness, for their zeal in being involved in the collection. We should look for opportunities to give, not simply wait for the situation to find us. Be intentional in giving.

A third principle in the attitude of giving is to give cheerfully: Christians are like their God when they find joy and gladness in giving.[77] There should be a joy, an inner rejoicing, when the opportunity to give arises. There is an implied contrast between "not grudgingly ... [but] cheerful[ly]." The Greek word for grudgingly typically refers to grief or sorrow, and in this text it refers to giving reluctantly. The contrast to giving sorrowfully is to give cheerfully.

---

77 There are some legitimate issues as to what it means that God "loves" this attitude in giving. See David E. Garland, *2 Corinthians*, New American Commentary, vol. 29 (Nashville: Broadman & Holman, 1999), 407.

We should be focusing on the honor we have to be allowed to partake in the collection, that God has blessed us so we can give to help the cause of Christ. It is a moment for rejoicing, not sadness that money is leaving our bank account.

⚹ The final concept is willingness: all of a Christian's possessions should be at the Lord's disposal. The problem the ruler had in Luke 18:18-24[78] is that he did not want to use his possessions for the glory of God, but for the comfort and glory of himself. Paul gives Timothy a command to teach the rich about some of the dangers associated with accumulated wealth, including the temptation to have hope in the riches of this world (1 Timothy 6:17-19). We should be a good steward over our possessions, but at the same time be willing to use all of them for God's glory.

THE AMOUNT OF GIVING

This is where the rubber meets the road, the moment of truth where all the principles discussed above are appropriately applied to our lives or are ignored. The question everyone seems to want to talk about is: "how much do I *need* to give?" However, to answer that question is to answer a bad question! Sometimes a question can reveal the heart-disposition of the one asking it. In this question the disposition seems to be: "how little can I give and not be sinning?" Why would anyone even want to know that answer?

Christianity is not very formulaic. A person is not saved by repeating special words, and the amount a certain Christian should give cannot be answered by the use of a calculator alone. In fact, the question of "how much" has been the direction of this entire chapter, because before "how much" can be answered, one needs to grasp the principles related to the driving force of giving, the motivations for giving, the details of giving, and proper attitude of giving. Only then has the proper foundation been laid to appropriately answer the "how much" question.

---

78 Cf. parallel passages in Matthew 19:16-21 and Mark 10:17-22.

There are four principles that must be followed. Now, some readers may finish this section and be disappointed. Why? Because there is no formula! However, when these four concepts are combined with the previous teaching in this chapter, the synergistic impact typically leads to Christians asking themselves: where can I cut my budget so I can give more to God's work?

First, the amount given is based upon income. The value of the contribution is expected to be related to the income of the one giving it.[79] This principle can be seen in a few passages. In the Old Testament, Moses said that every man should give something when he appears before the Lord during the three main festivals (Passover, Pentecost, and Tabernacles). However, the specific gift was not prescribed, but was to be "according to the blessing the LORD your God has given you" (Deuteronomy 16:17, HCSB). Paul says it very similarly in 1 Corinthians 16:2, declaring that the amount of the gift is to be based on "the extent that God has blessed you" (NET). In 2 Corinthians 8:12, Paul declares that a gift is acceptable based upon what a giver has since God does not expect them to give what he hasn't blessed them with.

Therefore, the greater one has been blessed, the greater proportion the gift should be. The percentage of income given by someone making $20,000 per year should be lower than someone making $60,000 per year. However, a helpful analysis compiled by Empty Tomb on 2005 incomes shows that this is not happening in the United States. The general trend is that the higher the income bracket, the lower the percentage of giving to charitable causes.[80] This trend demonstrates the exact opposite of the principle of income-based giving. Therefore, before deciding on an amount to give, recognize that as your income increases, your percentage of giving should increase as well.

A second consideration when deciding on the amount to give is the needs of those ministering to you and the needs of fellow

---

79 This is typically called "proportionate giving."
80 See Empty Tomb, Inc., "Income Bracket Highlights," < http://www. emptytomb.org/05cesincome.html > (accessed on July 31, 2012).

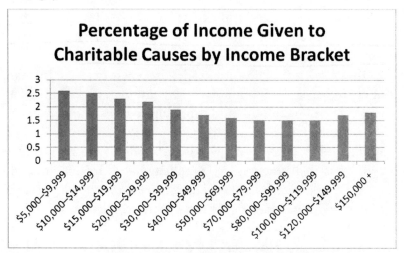

Percentage of Income Given to Charitable Causes by Income Bracket

saints. 1 Corinthians 9:1-14 explains that preachers of the gospel have the right to be supported (cf. Galatians 6:6). Therefore, the needs of the pastoral staff[81] at your church should be considered when giving. However, note that "needs" and "wants" are not the same. This principle does not justify a minister making an exorbitant amount of money; that is not required by 1 Corinthians 9. In fact, one of the qualifications of an elder is that he is not a lover of money (1 Timothy 3:3) or not greedy for gain (Titus 1:7). In many churches in America, the church leadership presents a budget to the congregation for their approval. Once the budget is approved, every Christian in that church is agreeing to help meet the giving needs required in that budget.

The needs of other saints must be considered as well. Twice in 2 Corinthians Paul mentions this concept. First, in 8:13-14, Paul says that God supplied an abundance of resources to the Corinthians in order for them to meet the need of the saints in Jerusalem. Second, in 9:12, he explicitly refers to the collection being used

---

81 The idea that the "pastoral staff" should be considered is one application of this text, which refers generally to "those who preach the gospel" (1 Corinthians 9:14, HCSB). Some interpreters may conclude that the reference is more narrow (e.g., only travelling evangelists), but I think it is more general.

for "supplying the needs of the saints" (HCSB). Therefore, when deciding on an amount to give, consider those ministering to you, the church budget, and the needs of fellow Christians.

The third principle to consider is generosity: a Christian should give generously, but not to the point of personal affliction. There is a fine line to walk in this principle, as Paul renders praise for the Macedonians because they gave "beyond their ability" (2 Corinthians 8:3, HCSB). The word translated "generosity" in 8:2 is usually translated "sincerity" or "simplicity." New Testament scholar David Garland helpfully explains its meaning in this context: "It comes to mean generosity as those with a singleness of concern for another's need stand ready to help."[82] This is surely a generous and sacrificial gift. However, the concept of generous should be tempered with wisdom, as Paul says that he does not want "relief for others and hardship for" the Corinthians (2 Corinthians 8:13, HCSB). I have personally seen friends give so much to those in need that they turned to their own church for financial help. Paul is warning against this kind of unwise giving. Therefore, consider how generous your giving is when deciding on an amount to contribute.

The final principle is that the amount is to be heart-based: giving is determined upon the amount decided in one's heart. Several texts can be considered here, but one from the Old Testament and one from the New will suffice. In Exodus 25, God tells Moses to raise a contribution from the people of Israel in order to make a sanctuary. When Moses speaks to Israel, he asks those "whose heart is willing" (Exodus 35:5, HCSB) to participate in the contribution. The description of the generosity of the Israelites is telling: "everyone whose heart was moved … all who had willing hearts" (Exodus 35:21-22, HCSB). This contribution, which came from the heart of the Israelites, was so overwhelmingly generous, that in Exodus 36:6 Moses commanded all contributions for the sanctuary to cease. In 2 Corinthians 9:7, Paul tells his audience that a Christian should give "as he has decided in his heart" (HCSB). The standard Greek lexicon explains this phrase as meaning "as he has

---

82 Garland, *2 Corinthians*, 367.

made up his mind."[83] As New Testament scholar Paul Barnett has concluded: "Careful prior deliberation by the giver is implied by these instructions."[84] God wants us to dedicate ourselves to Him first (2 Corinthians 8:5), and God will then move our hearts and lead us in generous, sacrificial giving.

CONCLUSION

The driving force of giving is the grace of God, our relationship with God, and God's love for us. The motivations for giving include expressing our thankfulness to God for all he has done, a desire to grow spiritually and be more like his Son, Jesus Christ, the joy of hearing praise from our Heavenly Father, and the knowledge that a future reward awaits us in Christ Jesus. Certain details that need to be considered when giving include the idea that all Christians should be involved in giving, that we should give systematically, and precautions should be taken with the handling of the collection. The attitude of giving is extremely important, as we should give voluntarily, not under compulsion. We should be intentional in our giving, and it should be done cheerfully and willingly. Once all of these principles are taken into consideration, the amount can be decided upon. At this point, we should be ready to sacrifice comfort, ready to give up luxuries, and ready to demonstrate our absolute gratefulness for all God has done for us through the work of Jesus on the cross. The amount should be decided by looking at our level of income, the needs of those ministering to us and of fellow saints, what a generous and sacrificial gift would be, and it should come from the heart.

You might be wondering if I have any specific suggestions as to an amount or a percentage of income. The reason for any hesitancy is that if I were to suggest that all Christians who make more than $100,000 dollars per year should give 20 percent of their income,

---

83 Bauer, *Greek-English Lexicon*, 865.
84 Paul Barnett, *The Second Epistle to the Corinthians*, NICNT (Grand Rapids: Eerdmans, 1997), 437.

I could be limiting their generosity. Maybe some would seek the Lord and pray about it and decide to give 40 percent of their income, but they don't find that necessary since only 20 percent was suggested. One couple told me after hearing this teaching that the Lord moved upon their hearts to increase their giving from 10 percent to 30 percent.

Some might look at their situation of debt, recognize that they are in debt due to sinful, materialistic decisions, and decide to change their lifestyle. They may decide that they have not truly shown their thankfulness to God by the way they contribute to their local church. These principles might apply differently for them than for others.

Also, another group might be in debt due to some tragedy, maybe a medical emergency or maybe they were defrauded out of a large sum of money. I knew one man who faced one million dollars in medical bills in order to save his son's life, and that was after the insurance had paid their portion. What does sacrificial, generous, heart-based giving look like to someone in that kind of debt? While no specific percentage or amount could be prescribed, wisdom, trust in the Lord, and obedience to the principles in Scripture are paramount in these situations. So, examine your heart, look at how you are currently spending money,[85] meditate on the grace and love of God, and ask for God's wisdom and direction as you first seek Him, and then seek to bring glory to Him through giving.

---

85 Maybe even ask a wise, trusted friend to review with you how you spend your money to see if there is anything that he believes is unwise.

Categories of Application

The Driving Force of Giving

Principle	Description	Location
Grace-Driven	Giving is a response to the grace of God shown to believers	2 Cor 8-9
Relationship-Driven	Giving is based upon one's relationship with the Lord and the receiver of the giving	2 Cor 8:5
Love-Driven	Giving is a demonstration of a Christians' love	2 Cor 8:8-9

The Motivations for Giving

Principle	Description	Location
Thankfulness	Giving expresses thankfulness to God	2 Cor 9:12
Spiritual growth	Giving causes one to grow in good works	2 Cor 9:6, 8
God's Praise	Recognize that God praises sacrificial giving	Mark 12:42-44; 2 Cor 8:2-3
Rewards	Not storing up for rewards here, but for eternal rewards	Matt 6:19-21

The Details of Giving

Principle	Description	Location
Universal	Every believer should give	1 Cor 16:2; Rom 1:20-21
Systematic	Give on a regular basis, that is, weekly, bi-monthly, or monthly	1 Cor 16:2
Precautions	Proper precautions should be made with the handling of money	2 Cor 8:20-21

The Attitude of Giving and Possessions

Principle	Description	Location
Voluntary	Giving ought to be done out of one's free volition	2 Cor 8:3; 9:7
Intentional	Seek opportunities and give deliberately in order to meet a genuine need, not out of guilt merely to soothe a pressing request	2 Cor 8:4; 9:2
Cheerfully	God loves a cheerful giver	2 Cor 9:7
Willingness	All of a Christian's possessions should be at the Lord's disposal	Matt 19:16-21

The Amount of Giving

Principle	Description	Location
Income-Based[86]	The value of the gift given is expected to be related to the income of the offerer	Deut 16:16-17; 1 Cor 16:2; 2 Cor 8:3, 12
Needs-Based	Meet the needs of those ministering and of fellow saints	1 Cor 9:1-14; 2 Cor 8:13-14; 2 Cor 9:12
Generous	Give generously, but not to the point of personal affliction	2 Cor 8:2-3, 13; Phil 4:17-18
Heart-Based	Giving is based upon the amount determined in one's heart	Exod 25:1; 35:5, 21-22; 36:6; 2 Cor 9:7

---

86 Usually referred to as the principle of proportionate giving.

BIBLIOGRAPHY

Alcorn, Randy. *Law of Rewards: Giving What You Can't Keep to Gain What You Can't Lose*. Wheaton: Tyndale, 2003.

_____. *Money, Possessions, and Eternity*. Wheaton: Tyndale, 1989.

Anderson, James Edward. "Priorities in Christian Giving." Th.M. thesis, Dallas Theological Seminary, 1967.

Aycock, Jarrette. *Tithing-Your Questions Answer*. Kansas City: Beacon Hill, 1955.

Babbs, Arthur V. *The Law of the Tithe: As Set Forth in the Old Testament*. New York: Revell, 1912.

Barndollar, W. W. "Scriptural Tithe." Th.D. diss., Grace Theological Seminary, 1959.

Barnett, Paul. *The Second Epistle to the Corinthians*. NICNT. Grand Rapids: Eerdmans, 1997.

Barrick, William D. "The Mosaic Covenant." Master's Seminary Journal 10, no. 2 (Fall 1999): 213-232.

Bauer, Walter. *A Greek-English Lexicon of the New Testament and Other Early Christian Literature*. 3rd ed. Revised and edited by F. W. Danker, W. F. Arndt, and F. W. Gingrich. Chicago: University of Chicago Press, 2000.

Berghoef, Gerard, and Lester DeKoster. *God's Yardstick*. Grand Rapids: Christian's Library, 1980.

Blomberg, Craig L. "Degrees of Reward in the Kingdom of Heaven." *JETS* 35 (1992): 159-72.

_____. *Matthew*, New American Commentary. Vol. 22. Nashville: Broadman & Holman Publishers, 2001.

Brown, Francis, S. R. Driver, and Charles A. Briggs. *A Hebrew and English Lexicon of the Old Testament*, trans. by Edward Robinson. Oxford: Clarendon Press, 1906.

Burkett, Larry. *Giving and Tithing*. Chicago: Moody, 1991.

Burroughs, P. E. *The Grace of Giving*. Nashville: Sunday School Board of the Southern Baptist Convention, 1934.

Campbell, Ken M. "What Was Jesus' Occupation?" *Journal of the Evangelical Theological Society* 48:3 (2005): 502-19.

Carson, D. A. *Exegetical Fallacies*, 2d ed. Grand Rapids: Baker, 1996.

Clearwaters, Richard V. *Stewardship Sermonettes*. Grand Rapids: Baker, 1955.

Cook, Charles A. *Systematic Giving: The Church's Safeguard against Nineteenth Century Evils*. Philadelphia: American Baptist Publication Society, 1903.

Cove, Morgan. *An Essay on the Revenues of the Church of England: With An Inquiry into the Necessity, Justice, and Policy of an Abolition or Commutation of Tithes*, 3d. London: F. C. and J. Rivington, 1816.

Crawford, Julius Earl. *The Call to Christian Stewardship*. Nashville: M. E. South, 1926.

Croteau, David A. *You Mean I Don't Have to Tithe? A Deconstruction of Tithing and a Reconstruction of Post-Tithe Giving*. Eugene, OR: Pickwick, 2010.

_____. ed. *Perspectives on Tithing: 4 Views*. Nashville: Broadman & Holman, 2011.

Cushman, Ralph S., and Martha F. Bellinger. *Adventures in Stewardship*. New York: Abingdon, 1919.

DeMar, Gary. *God and Government: Issues in Biblical Perspective*. Vol. 2. Brentwood, TN: Wolgemuth & Hyatt, 1989.

Dillard, J. E., ed. *Building a Stewardship Church: A Handbook for Church Workers*. 2d ed. Nashville: Southern Baptist Convention, 1947.

_____. *Good Stewards*. Nashville: Broadman, 1953.

Dodd, Monroe E. *Concerning the Collection: A Manual for Christian Stewardship*. New York: Revell, 1929.

Duncan, John Wesley. *Our Christian Stewardship*. New York: Eaton & Mains, 1909.

Ellingworth, Paul. *The Epistle to the Hebrews: A Commentary on the Greek Text*. NIGTC. Grand Rapids: Eerdmans, 1993.

Empty Tomb, Inc. "Income Bracket Highlights." < www.empty-tomb.org/05cesincome.html >. Accessed on July 31, 2012.

Freeman, John D. *More Than Money*. Nashville: Sunday School Board of the Southern Baptist Convention, 1935.

Foshee, Howard. "The Tithe." In *Encyclopedia of Southern Baptists*. Edited by Norman Wade Cox. 2 vols. Nashville: Broadman, 1958.

Garland, David E. *2 Corinthians*. New American Commentary. Vol. 29. Nashville: Broadman & Holman, 1999.

Gill, Ben. *Stewardship: The Biblical Basis for Living*. Arlington: Summit, 1996.

Gonzalez, Justo. *Faith and Wealth*. San Francisco: Harper, 1990.

Gordon, A. J. *God's Tenth*. Richmond: Foreign Mission Board, Southern Baptist Convention, [1880s]), 2-3.

Gough, John. *Tracts on Tithes*. Dublin: Jackson, 1786.

Grant, Frederick C. *The Economic Background of the Gospels*. London: Oxford, 1926.

Grindstaff, W. E. *Principles of Stewardship Development*. Nashville: Convention Press, 1967.

Hanegraaff, Hank. *The Bible Answer Book*. Nashville: J. Countryman, 2004.

Harrell, Costen J. *Stewardship and the Tithe*. New York: Abingdon, 1953.

Harshman, Charles William. *Christian Giving*. New York: Eaton and Mains, 1905.

Hastings, Robert J. *My Money and God*. Nashville: Broadman, 1961.

Hays, J. Daniel. "Applying the Old Testament Law Today." *Bibliotheca Sacra* 158: 629 (2001): 21-35.

Hensey, James A. *Storehouse Tithing or Stewardship-Up-To-Date*. New York: Revell, 1922.

Hobbs, Herschel H. *The Gospel of Giving*. Nashville: Broadman, 1954.

Holmes, Charley. "Tithing: A Timeless Moral Imperative or Old Testament Legalism?" D.Min. dissertation, Reformed Theological Seminary, 1998.

Instone-Brewer, David. *Prayer and Agriculture*. Traditions of Rabbis from the Era of the New Testament. Vol. 1. Grand Rapids: Eerdmans, 2004.

I Tithe Joyfully! A book of Letters from Those Who Do. Chicago: Moody, 1960.

James, David M. "Christian Giving." *Living Orthodoxy* 21, no. 4 (2000): 8.

[Kane, Thomas]. "What We Owe and Why We Owe It." In *Tithing and Its Results*. Chicago: The Layman Company, 1915.

Kauffman, Milo. *The Challenge of Christian Stewardship*. Scottdale, PA: Herald Press, 1955.

Kendall, Robert T. *Tithing: A Call to Serious, Biblical Giving*. Grand Rapids: Zondervan, 1982.

Lansdell, Henry. *The Sacred Tenth or Studies in Tithe-Giving Ancient and Modern*. 2 vols. 1906. Reprint, 2 vols. in 1. Grand Rapids: Baker, 1955.

Lea, Thomas D., and Hayne P. Griffin. *1, 2 Timothy, Titus.* New American Commentary. Vol. 34. Nashville: Broadman & Holman Publishers, 2001.

Leavell, Frank H. *Training in Stewardship.* Nashville: Sunday School Board Southern Baptist Convention, 1920.

Lenski, R. C. H. *The Interpretation of St. Paul's First and Second Epistle to the Corinthians.* Columbus: Wartburg, 1946.

Lovejoy, Luther E. *Stewardship for All of Life.* Life and Service Series. New York: Methodist Book Concern, 1924.

Lowry, Oscar. *Should Christians Tithe?* Fort Wayne: Glad Tidings, [1940s].

MacCulloch, J. A. "Tithes." In *Encyclopaedia of Religion and Ethics.* Edited by James Hastings. New York: Scribner, 1951.

Mathews, Kenneth A. *Genesis 1-11:26.* New American Commentary. Vol. 1A. Nashville: Broadman & Holman Publishers, 2001.

May, John Albert. *The Law of God on Tithes and Offerings or God's Plan to Finance His Church.* 3d ed., rev. and enl. Nashville: M. E. Church, 1919.

Mitchell, John J. "Tithing, Yes!" *Presbyterian Guardian* 47 (October 1978): 6.

Moore, Merrill D. *Found Faithful: Christian Stewardship in Personal and Church Life.* Nashville: Broadman, 1953.

Morley, Brian K. "Tithe, Tithing." In *Evangelical Dictionary of Biblical Theology.* Edited by Walter A. Elwell. Grand Rapids: Baker, 1996.

Morris, Leon. *The Gospel According to Matthew.* Grand Rapids: Eerdmans, 1992.

Mueller, John Theodore. *Christian Dogmatics: A Handbook of Doctrinal Theology for Pastors, Teachers, and Laymen.* St. Louis: Concordia, 1934.

Muncy, Jr., W. L. *Fellowship with God through Christian Steward-ship*. Kansas City: Central Seminary Press, 1949.

Murray, Stuart. *Beyond Tithing*. Carlisle, UK: Paternoster, 2000.

Olford, Stephen. *The Grace of Giving: Thoughts on Financial Stew-ardship*. Grand Rapids: Zondervan, 1972.

Paschall, H. Franklin. "Tithing in the New Testament." In *Resource Unlimited*, ed. William L. Hendricks. Nashville: Stewardship Commission of the Southern Baptist Convention, 1972.

[Peck, Kenrick]. *The Universal Obligation of Tithes*. London: Elliot Stock, 1901.

Peterson, Orval D. *Stewardship in the Bible. Bethany Study Course.* St. Louis: Bethany, 1952.

Pink, Arthur W. *Tithing*. Swengel, PA: Reiner, 1967.

Powell, Luther P. *Money and the Church.* New York: Association Press, 1962.

Powers, Thomas J. "An Historical Study of the Tithe in the Christian Church to 1648." Ph.D. diss., Southern Baptist Theological Seminary, 1948.

Rees, Tom. *Money Talks*. Frinton-on-Sea, Essex, UK: Hildenbor-ough Hall, [1960-1980].

Rice, John R. *All about Christian Giving.* Wheaton: Sword of the Lord, 1954.

Rigby, N. L. *Christ Our Creditor: "How Much Owest Thou?" or The Tithe Terumoth: Its Philosophy, History and Perpetuity.* Murray, KY: News and Truth Publishing, [1895-1899].

Robertson, Archibald T. "Paul's Plans for Raising Money." In *Clas-sic Sermons on Stewardship*, compiled by Warren W. Wiersbe. Kregel Classic Sermons. Grand Rapids: Kregel, 1999.

Robertson, A. T. *Five Times Five Points of Church Finance.* 2d ed. Lima: n.p., 1886.

Rouse, W. H. D. "Tithes (Greek)." In *Encyclopædia of Religion and Ethics*, ed. James Hastings. New York: Scribner, 1951.

Salstrand, George A. E. *The Tithe: The Minimum Standard for Christian Giving.* Grand Rapids: Baker, 1952.

Sarna, Nahum M. *Genesis.* The JPS Torah Commentary. Philadelphia: Jewish Publication Society, 1989.

Shaw, S. B. *God's Financial Plan or Temporal Prosperity: The Result of Faithful Stewardship.* Chicago: Shaw, 1897.

Simpson, John E. *"He That Giveth:" A Study of the Stewardship of Money as Taught in* Scripture. New York: Revell, 1935.

Speer, William. *God's Rule for Christian Giving: A Practical Essay on the Science of Christian Economy.* Philadelphia: Presbyterian Board of Publication, 1875.

Spruce, Fletcher Clarke. *You Can Be a Joyful Tither.* Kansas City: Beacon Hill, 1966.

Stanley, Charles. *The Glorious Journey.* Nashville: Nelson, 1996.

Stein, Robert H. *Luke.* New American Commentary. Vol. 24. Nashville: Broadman & Holman, 2001.

Stewart, E. B. *The Tithe.* Chicago: Winona Publishing, 1903.

Thayer, Joseph Henry. *A Greek-English Lexicon of the New Testament.* New York: American Book Company, 1889.

Thompson, P. W. *The Whole Tithe.* London: Marshall Brothers, [1920].

Turner, David, and Darrell L. Bock. *Matthew and Mark.* Cornerstone Biblical Commentary. Vol. 11. Carol Stream, IL: Tyndale House Publishers, 2005.

Verhoef, Pieter. "Tithing: A Hermeneutical Consideration." In *The Law and the Prophets: Old Testament Studies Prepared in Honor of O. T. Allis,* ed. John H. Skilton. Phillipsburg: Presbyterian & Reformed, 1974.

Watley, William D. *Bring the Full Tithe: Sermons on the Grace of Giving.* Valley Forge: Judson, 1995.

Watson, George D. *Soul Food: Being Chapters on the Interior Life with Passages of Personal Experience.* Cincinnati: Knapp, 1896.

Wester, Brooks H. "The Christian and the Tithe." In *Classic Sermons on Stewardship*, compiled by Warren W. Wiersbe. Kregel Classic Sermons. Grand Rapids: Kregel, 1999.

Williams, Leewin B. *Financing the Kingdom*. Grand Rapids: Eerdmans, 1945.

Young, Samuel. *Giving and Living: Foundations for Christian Stewardship*. 1974. Reprint, Grand Rapids: Baker, 1976.

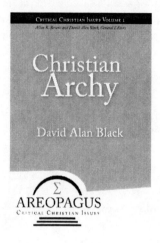
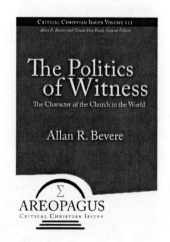

MORE FROM ENERGION PUBLICATIONS

Personal Study

Finding My Way in Christianity	Herold Weiss	$16.99
Holy Smoke! Unholy Fire	Bob McKibben	$14.99
The Jesus Paradigm	David Alan Black	$17.99
When People Speak for God	Henry Neufeld	$17.99
The Sacred Journey	Chris Surber	$11.99

Christian Living

Faith in the Public Square	Robert D. Cornwall	$16.99
Grief: Finding the Candle of Light	Jody Neufeld	$8.99
Crossing the Street	Robert LaRochelle	$16.99

Bible Study

Learning and Living Scripture	Lentz/Neufeld	$12.99
From Inspiration to Understanding	Edward W. H. Vick	$24.99
Luke: A Participatory Study Guide	Geoffrey Lentz	$8.99
Philippians: A Participatory Study Guide	Bruce Epperly	$9.99
Ephesians: A Participatory Study Guide	Robert D. Cornwall	$9.99

Theology

Creation in Scripture	Herold Weiss	$12.99
Creation: the Christian Doctrine	Edward W. H. Vick	$12.99
The Politics of Witness	Allan R. Bevere	$9.99
Ultimate Allegiance	Robert D. Cornwall	$9.99
History and Christian Faith	Edward W. H. Vick	$9.99
The Church Under the Cross	William Powell Tuck	$11.99
The Journey to the Undiscovered Country	William Powell Tuck	$9.99
Eschatology: A Participatory Study Guide	Edward W. H. Vick	$9.99

Ministry

Clergy Table Talk	Kent Ira Groff	$9.99
Out of This World	Darren McClellan	$24.99

Generous Quantity Discounts Available
Dealer Inquiries Welcome
Energion Publications — P.O. Box 841
Gonzalez, FL_ 32560
Website: http://energionpubs.com
Phone: (850) 525-3916

CPSIA information can be obtained at www.ICGtesting.com
Printed in the USA
LVOW11s0810050116

469120LV00001B/20/P